THE REVISED VERSION
EDITED FOR THE USE OF SCHOOLS

THE
BOOK OF EXODUS

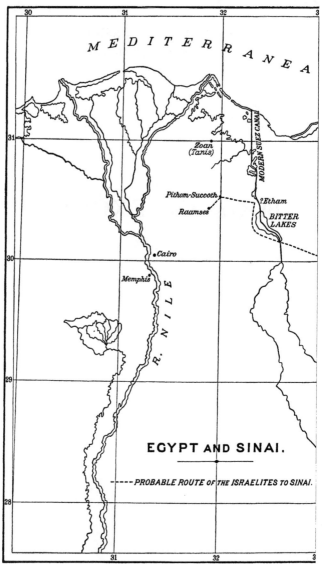

MEDITERRANEA N E A

Zoan
(Tanis)

MODERN SUEZ CANAL

Pithom-Succooth

Raamses

?Etham

BITTER
LAKES

•Cairo

Memphis

R. NILE

EGYPT AND SINAI.

------PROBABLE ROUTE OF THE ISRAELITES TO SINAI.

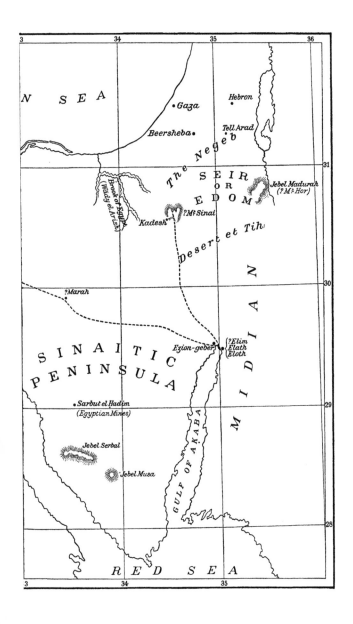

THE
BOOK OF EXODUS

BY

L. ELLIOTT BINNS, B.D.

EDITOR OF 'JEREMIAH' (WESTMINSTER COMMENTARIES)
AUTHOR OF 'ERASMUS THE REFORMER'
(HULSEAN LECTURES) ETC.

CAMBRIDGE
AT THE UNIVERSITY PRESS
1924

CAMBRIDGE
UNIVERSITY PRESS

University Printing House, Cambridge CB2 8BS, United Kingdom

Published in the United States of America by Cambridge University Press, New York

Cambridge University Press is part of the University of Cambridge.

It furthers the University's mission by disseminating knowledge in the pursuit of
education, learning and research at the highest international levels of excellence.

www.cambridge.org
Information on this title: www.cambridge.org/9781107670280

© Cambridge University Press 1924

First published 1924
First paperback edition 2014

A catalogue record for this publication is available from the British Library

ISBN 978-1-107-67028-0 Paperback

PREFACE BY THE GENERAL EDITOR
FOR THE OLD TESTAMENT

THE aim of this series of commentaries is to explain the Revised Version for young students, and at the same time to present, in a simple form, the main results of the best scholarship of the day.

The General Editor has confined himself to supervision and suggestion. The writer is, in each case, responsible for the opinions expressed and for the treatment of particular passages.

A. H. M^cNEILE.

DUBLIN, 1923.

CONTENTS

PAGE

MAP (EGYPT AND SINAI) . . . . *Frontispiece*

INTRODUCTION 1–18

  1. The Title of the Book and its position in the
     Canon 1

  2. The Sources and Literary Structure . . 1

  3. The Historical Value of the Book . . 5

  4. The Religious Value of the Book . . 8

  5. The Legislation in Exodus 10

  6. The Tabernacle 13

  7. The History of Contemporary Egypt . . 15

  8. Analysis 17

TEXT AND NOTES 19–144

INDEX 145–148

INTRODUCTION

1. The Title of the Book and its position in the Canon.

The name for the book among the Hebrews was We'ēleh Shemōth, its title being derived from the first few words of the original in accordance with the usual manner of referring to books amongst the Hebrews. The title in our English Bible comes from the Vulgate *Exodus*, which in its turn was taken from LXX Ἔξοδος. Exodus is the second book of the *Torah* or Law, the first division of the Hebrew Canon or list of sacred writings. It is usual to refer to the five books which make up this division as the Pentateuch.

In Exodus the history of the Hebrew people is continued from the death of Joseph (i. 8) to the commencement of the second year of the wanderings (xl. 1, 17) which found the tribes encamped in the wilderness of Sinai around the newly erected tabernacle.

2. The Sources and Literary Structure.

Tradition has ascribed the authorship of the Pentateuch to Moses. It should however be remembered that the books themselves give no hint of this ascription; on the contrary, since Moses is referred to in the third person and even his death is described (Deut. xxxiv. 5 ff.), their evidence, at first sight at any rate, is inconsistent with it. The possibility of the closing portion of Deut. being an addition must not however be ignored, nor is the custom of an author's referring to himself in the third person entirely unknown. It is hard to conceive however that passages like Exod. xi. 3 and Numb. xii. 3 can have come from Moses himself. On the other hand, though we may question the Mosaic authorship of the books of the Pentateuch as they now exist, it would be difficult to deny them a Mosaic kernel around which later additions have been formed.

A careful examination of the Pentateuch, especially if it be conducted in the original Hebrew, almost inevitably suggests that whoever gave the final form to the books and whenever this stage of their development was reached, many documents or oral traditions were combined in them; and further, that these traditions whether oral or written had their origins amongst people of different points of view and living in widely separated generations. It will perhaps be well to give a few instances of narratives or incidents which appear more than once in the story and also of some which seem definitely to disagree the one with the other. The call of Moses is twice given (iii. 2 ff. and vi. 2 ff.), as is the story of the quails (xvi. and Numb. xi.) and that of the striking of the rock (xvii. 1 ff. and Numb. xx. 1–13). It may be that such incidents did actually occur more than once, a possible explanation also of the twofold appointment of Moses' co-adjutors (xviii. 21 ff. and Numb. xi. 14 ff.), but such repetitions are so frequent and so similar in detail that some other explanation seems to be necessary. Furthermore, in certain of these repetitions the subject would seem to be considered from entirely different standpoints. Examples of this are to be found in the matter of the speaking powers of Moses (cf. iv. 10 ff. with viii. 9 f., 26 f., etc.); the agent by whom the wonders were wrought—in vii. 8, 20, viii. 5, 16, ix. 8, xii. 1 (all P) this agent is Aaron, in vii. 14, viii. 1, 20, ix. 1, 13, 22, x. 1, 12, 21 (all JE) it is Moses; in xvi. 31 the manna tasted like wafers made with honey, in Numb. xi. 8 like fresh oil; in xxxviii. 25 f. the census has already taken place, but according to Numb. i. it was still to be made. Other instances of different traditions may be found in the name of Moses' father-in-law, and also in the name of the sacred mountain (Sinai in J and P, Horeb in D and E).

That the Pentateuch was made up of different documents or sources would be admitted I think by all schools of critics; the difficulty arises when the attempt is made to arrange these various sources into groups and to trace their origins. The system which in broad outline has been accepted by the large majority of scholars in recent years is that generally associated with the name of Wellhausen. This system would divide up the Pentateuchal sources into four main groups, known as J, E, D, and P. There is in addition a smaller source known as the Law of Holiness (H) which underlies Lev. xvii.–xxvi., traces of whose influence can be found here and there in the rest of the Pentateuch.

The four main sources belong to different ages of the Hebrew people, though it must be remembered that any dates which we may assign to them are only approximate and are not intended to rule out the inclusion of much earlier matter or even the addition of later accretions. The latest source is that known as the Priestly (P), which McNeile would date from 500 to 300 B.C. This source is greatly interested in the origins of religious institutions and in matters of ritual; it is fond of using set forms of words and takes delight in preserving detailed statements of measurements and distances. A few of its characteristic words and phrases are the following:

> *between the two evenings*: xii. 6 (see note), xvi. 12, xxix. 39, 41, xxx. 8. Six times elsewhere, all in P.

> *congregation* (עֵדָה): used in a technical sense it appears 115 times, all of them in P or in H, which has many of the characteristics of P.

offer, lit. *bring near* (הִקְרִיב): very frequent in P, H and in Ezekiel.

plague, lit. *striking* (נֶגֶף): xii. 13, xxx. 12, and five times elsewhere, all of them P except Isa. viii. 14.

tribe, lit. *staff* (מַטֶּה): xxxi. 2, 6, xxxv. 30, 34, etc. Never found in JE or D.

The next source in point of time is the Deuteronomic (D), which is so called from the book of that name. The traces of its influence in Exodus are but slight and consist of a few phrases exhorting the people to obedience and to the exhibition of kindliness: see xii. 25 ff., xiii. 3–9, 14–16, xv. 26, xix. 3–6. The date according to McNeile is from about 600 to 550 B.C.

The two remaining sources, the Jahvistic (J) and the Elohistic (E) are so called because of their preference for the different names for the God of Israel, in the one the personal name, Jehovah (or better, Jahweh; see on iii. 2) is used, in the other up to Exod. iii. 14 the general term for God, Elohim. The source J probably came from Judah and reached its final form about 800 B.C., whilst E, which came from the Northern kingdom, is slightly later. At a comparatively early date these sources were combined into a single history (JE), and as they have many characteristics in common it is often quite impossible to separate them with any certainty. When compared with P both are simpler and more natural in style and have a more primitive outlook on life and religion: they contain the earliest traditions of the Hebrew people. The following are some of the few marks which distinguish them:

(a) Characteristics of J.

Preference for the name *Jahweh.*

to find grace or favour (מָצָא חֵן): xxxiii. 12 f., 16, xxxiv. 9. Fifteen times elsewhere in J, once in D and once in P.

flowing with milk and honey: iii. 8, 17, xiii. 5, xxxiii. 3.
In J four times elsewhere, seven in D, once in H.

harden, lit. *make heavy* (כבד): of Pharaoh's heart,
vii. 14, viii. 15, 32, ix. 7, 34, x. 1. Never in E or P.

(*b*) Characteristics of E.

Preference for *Elohim* (up to iii. 14).

Horeb used instead of *Sinai*.

Jethro for the priest of Midian: iii. 1, iv. 18, xviii. 1, etc.

Idiomatic use of בַּעַל (= *Master*) to express ownership
or property in: see xxi. 3 (with note), 22, 28 f., 34 f.,
36, xxii. 8, 11 f., 14 f., xxiv. 14, etc. Usage three
times in D, not in J or P.

By some critics the various sources have been analysed
still further and divided up into different strata. Such
divisions are not very convincing, as the evidence which
is supposed to support them is often mainly subjective.

Fuller details as to the sources of the book will be found
in the two excellent commentaries of McNeile (Westminster Series) and Driver (Cambridge Bible), as well as in
Chapman's *Introduction to the Pentateuch* (Cambridge
Bible), in which references to larger works such as Car-
penter and Harford, *The Composition of the Hexateuch*,
will be found.

3. THE HISTORICAL VALUE OF THE BOOK.

In past ages the narrative of Exodus was accepted as a
literal account, accurate even in the minutest details of the
events which took place in Egypt and in the wanderings,
and it was believed that this account came from the principal actor, Moses himself. As we saw in the previous
section such a view of the book is no longer held by the
great majority of scholars; on the contrary, it is regarded
as coming from a variety of periods, several of them much
later in time, and as having been affected by the ideas and
pre-suppositions of such periods.

If this is a true account of Exodus, as seems most likely, the question immediately arises as to whether it possesses any historical value at all. To this it may be replied that the historical value of the book is still as great as ever; for though it may not be a contemporary account of the sojourn in Egypt and of the deliverance therefrom, yet it gives very valuable insight into the religious ideas of a later age, and in those sections which come from P we are made acquainted with the longings and ideals of the post-exilic priesthood. The earlier sources have also preserved many primitive traditions of the Israelites and some even which go back into far past ages before the different branches of the Semitic stock had separated from one another.

The history itself in its broad outlines is unaffected by criticism. Three great historical phenomena are to be found in Exodus: (*a*) the sojourn in Egypt; (*b*) the deliverance and wanderings; (*c*) the work of a great leader and teacher. Round each of these three groups of facts many traditions and stories have gathered, but if in the light of modern research we are compelled to reject many of these, such a rejection does not involve the denial of the occurrences themselves.

(*a*) *The Sojourn in Egypt.* According to xii. 40 the children of Israel were in Egypt for 430 years. There are however grave difficulties in the way of accepting this figure since Moses and his contemporaries seem to have been the fourth generation only from Jacob; we may take it however that we are intended to suppose that the whole people was in Egypt for some considerable period. This tradition is so firmly planted in the mind of the Hebrew nation that it must certainly be based upon real facts. Is there any evidence in favour of it from sources outside the Bible? The testimony of Egyptian history is not absolutely clear, but it is at least probable that the *Aperu* mentioned in the inscriptions are of Hebrew race, or perhaps it would be safer to say included Hebrews amongst them, for we can hardly imagine that the Egyptians were at pains to distinguish very exactly between one Bedawin tribe and another. If all the children of Israel went into Egypt at the time of the famine there are reasons for supposing that some of them returned to Palestine soon afterwards, for "Israel" is included in the list of Canaanite peoples punished by Merenptah in 1220 B.C., shortly before the generally accepted date of the Exodus.

(b) *The Exodus.* The canonical book tells us that the whole of the people of Israel went out of Egypt accompanied by a mixed multitude (xii. 37 ff.). If however we accept the identification of the Hebrews with the *Aperu* of the inscriptions some of them must have been left behind in Egypt, since these people are mentioned in inscriptions as late as the reign of Rameses IV (1171–1165 B.C.). It should not be forgotten however that the writers of the Old Testament not infrequently speak in a general way, and in the long period which elapsed between the events themselves and the time when they were put into writing, the traditions of the various tribes and peoples who went to make up the later Israel may have been fused, and experiences which befell portions of the people only may have been referred to the whole.

(c) *The work of Moses.* If the Old Testament did not inform us of the existence of Moses, some great leader would have to be postulated in order to account for the development and rise of the Hebrew people. The book of Exodus shews him to us as a statesman consolidating and moulding the scattered tribes who fled from Egypt into a united nation; it shews him to us as a great teacher and prophet sent from God; and it shews him to us as a great lawgiver (cf. § 5). Modern critics accept him in all these capacities, though they may not accept in its entirety all that has been attributed to him by later tradition.

4. THE RELIGIOUS VALUE OF THE BOOK.

To the Jews history had above all else a didactic value, it was written in order to shew forth the wonders of God's dealings with His people : hence its supreme value for religion. This value is quite independent of the exact truth of the narrative in which the teaching is conveyed, since, as we saw in the previous section, a late account of an event may throw light on the ideas of the time in which it was put into writing. As a record óf men's aspirations after God and the gradual response of God to such aspirations the importance of the book is undiminished by the work of critics, nay, its value is increased, since the true perspective is restored.

The Old Testament is a vehicle for conveying to us the spiritual experiences of the Hebrew people and a record of the development amongst them of the knowledge of God. This being so we must not be surprised if we find in the different strata of Exodus conceptions of the divine nature and of religion which are by no means identical. The following are some of the main religious ideas of the book :

(a) *The idea of God.* Exodus contains two great passages in which the character of God is disclosed. In iii. 14, according to some of the greatest of recent scholars, the Name should be rendered I WILL BE WHAT I WILL BE, meaning that God's character will become known more and more fully as man's experience increases, the revelation unfolding with the evergrowing life of the race. When this conception of God is combined with the revelation of xxxiv. 6 f. we have an idea of God which is potentially capable of meeting all our needs.

To the Israelite Jehovah was the God of the ancestors of his race (iii. 16) with whom and with whose descendants He stood in covenant relation (vi. 4 f.). He is revealed in history as the guide and protector of His people, for whose welfare even the course of nature could be diverted according to the Hebrew interpretation of events (xiii. 21 f., xiv. 15 ff. etc.). He was accepted as the supreme God, though the existence of other deities might appear to be recognised in certain passages (xv. 11, xx. 3). At the same time primitive ideas concerning Him still existed, the crude anthropomorphisms which had survived amidst more spiritual conceptions ; Jehovah has to come down (iii. 8), He attacks men (iv. 24), He has bodily parts like a man (xxxiii. 22 f.). In other passages however God is represented as speaking from heaven (xx. 22) or as revealing Himself by means of inferior beings (iii. 2, xxiii. 20).

(*b*) *The duty of man.* (i) *Righteousness.* In the laws of Exodus (cf. § 5) we have the beginnings of social righteousness based on the requirements of a righteous and holy God (xxii. 31) with whom the Israelites stand in covenant relation (xxxiv. 10). The world was thus being prepared through the training of a selected nation for the much higher standard required in the New Testament.

The duty of man. (ii) *Worship.* God demands not only righteousness, but worship also (xxiv. 17 ff.). In those parts of the book which come from P an elaborate sacrificial system is described ; but it is not probable that this system was actually carried out in all its fulness at any period of Israel's history, certainly not during the wanderings in the wilderness; like the system described in the closing chapters of the book of Ezekiel we have here an attempt to represent the greatness of Jehovah and His separation from all that is unholy, "endeavours to give a fixed and permanent shape, according to the conditions of earthly life, to ideas which in their essential nature led the thoughts of men forward to the future and the unseen" (Westcott, *Hebrews*, p. 235).

The whole system was a permanent witness to the Presence of God in the midst of His people, to His holiness and hatred of sin, and to His desire that men should hold communion with Him. Such truths can never be over-emphasised and the Jewish system has still a value for us when spiritually interpreted, and not least of all as fore-shadowing the work of our Saviour (cf. the working out of this in the Epistle to the Hebrews).

5. The Legislation in Exodus.

The four later books of the Pentateuch as they stand at present contain various groups of laws all of which are attributed to Moses acting as the messenger of Jehovah. These various groups are attributed to four different periods: (*a*) the eve of the Exodus (Exod. xii, xxiii); (*b*) the sojourn before the Sacred Mountain (Exod. xx.–Numb. x. 10); (*c*) the wandering in the wilderness (Numb. xv. ff.); (*d*) the time immediately before the entry into Palestine (Deut.). Some of these laws come from the early sources JE, e.g. xx. 1–7, xx. 22–xxiii. 33 (the Book of the Covenant), xxxiv. 11–26 (the second decalogue), but the majority belong to P.

If the laws are arranged according to subject matter two principal divisions at once reveal themselves, (A) laws concerned with the religious or ceremonial life of the nation, (B) those intended to regulate social life. It must however be remembered that such a distinction had no meaning for the Hebrews; since the whole community was regarded as being under the direct rule of God Himself, all laws were equally sacred. The division between religious and secular had not yet arisen.

A. *Ceremonial Laws.* The following are some of the more important subjects dealt with.

(*a*) *The object of worship.* God alone is worthy of reverence (xx. 1, xxiii. 13, xxiv. 14) and in His worship the use of images is forbidden (xx. 2; cf. xxiii. 24, 32).

(*b*) *The method of worship.* In the early days worship was very simple and an altar of earth alone was to be used (xx. 24); but in the later regulations of P an exceedingly elaborate ritual is presupposed with much ecclesiastical furniture.

(*c*) *The sacred offerings.* To God belong the first fruits of men (xiii. 13), of beasts (xiii. 12), and of harvest (xxii. 29, xxxiv. 26). The later sacrificial system was elaborate and detailed; burnt offerings and peace offerings, sin offerings and guilt offerings being provided for (cf. xx. 24, xxix. 10 ff.).

(*d*) *The sacred seasons.* The older festivals were three in number and were connected with agricultural operations; Unleavened cakes (xxiii. 15, xxiv. 18), Weeks or Harvest (xxiii. 16, xxxiv. 22) and Ingathering or Booths (xxiii. 16, xxxiv. 22). The weekly Sabbath was also observed (xx. 8, xxiii. 12, xxxiv. 21). The keeping of the Passover was connected with the first of the three annual feasts (xii. 1 ff.)

B. *Social Laws.* These laws concern both the property and the persons of the Hebrews as well as the status of certain classes of people.

(*a*) *Injuries to Persons.* Murder (xxi. 12, 23) is to be punished with death, and so is the equally serious crime of kidnapping (xxi. 16). Various other cases of minor injury are also provided for (xxi. 18 ff.).

(*b*) *Injuries to Property.* These may arise through theft (xxiii. 1 ff.) or neglect to control beasts (xxii. 5) or by fire (xxii. 6).

(*c*) *Adultery and Impurity.* Adultery is of course forbidden by the Decalogue (xx. 14) and other forms of impurity and crimes against nature are also forbidden (xxii. 16 f., 19).

(*d*) *Slaves.* Slaves were regarded as the property of their master but his rights over them were restricted (xxi. 2–11); injury to the slave may mean his restoration to freedom (xxi. 26 f.). The position of the concubine was also protected (xxi. 7 ff.).

(*e*) *Land.* Private property in land is recognised, but the owner's power is not absolute since at certain periods the land must be allowed to lie fallow (xxiii. 10 f.).

(*f*) *Sojourners, widows, orphans.* These various classes being without natural protectors required special legislation on their behalf (xxii. 21 f., xxxiii. 9).

The punishments which were to follow breaches of any of the laws are of interest. God Himself would in certain cases be avenged upon the wrongdoer and even upon his children (xx. 5), but for the most part the law itself stated the punishment. The more serious crimes were followed by death (xxi. 12, 15, xxii. 18) or exile (xii. 15); for the lesser some form of compensation (xxi. 19, xxii. 17) or restitution (xxi. 33 f., xx. 5 f., 14 f.) sufficed. As amongst the Romans imprisonment formed no part of the penalty.

It has often been pointed out that the code of laws contained in the Pentateuch is far from complete and various suggestions have been made to account for this. Some think that a good deal of legal matter existed outside the Canonical books or that rulings would be given by the priests and other judges on disputed points. Possibly also much earlier matter has been lost owing to its having become obsolete and therefore not worthy of preservation. It may be that in many things the Hebrews when they settled in Canaan took over the legal system of the inhabitants or parts of it and that the Mosaic law was a supplement to that of the Canaanites. These latter, as we know from contemporary evidence like the Tell el-Amarna Tablets, were highly civilised and had been much influenced by the manners and customs of the Babylonians.

Perhaps the Hebrews had retained during their long exile some knowledge of their primitive home and its ways but more probably they recovered such knowledge for the most part through intercourse with the men of Canaan.

6. THE TABERNACLE.

A great part of the book of Exodus is occupied by a description of the Tabernacle and its contents; it will therefore be of some use to consider not only the structure itself, about which there is much that is obscure, but also its contents, and, further, its place in the life of the Hebrew people.

A. *The Structure and Contents.* The pattern of the tabernacle was revealed to Moses in the Mount (xxv. 9) and very full details are given to us. On approaching it the appearance was that of a court enclosed by curtains each hanging on poles or pillars of 5 cubits in height (that is about 7½ ft.). This outer court measured some 150 ft. by 75 ft. and in it were the altar of burnt offerings (xxvii. 1 ff.) and the brazen laver (xxx. 17 ff.). The tabernacle itself was a large tent or marquee supported by boards made of acacia wood (xxvi. 15–30) and having a triple depth of hangings; first curtains of tapestry (xxvi. 1–6), then hangings of goats' hair (xxvi. 7–13), and on top of all a covering of rams' skins and seal skins.

The tent was divided internally by a veil (xxvi. 31 ff.) into two unequal parts, the Holy Place (20 cubits by 10) and the Most Holy (10 cubits by 10). In the former were the table for the Shewbread (xxv. 23 ff.), the lampstand (xxv. 31 ff.) and the incense altar (xxx. 1–10). The Most Holy Place contained the Ark with the mercy seat and overshadowing Cherubim (xxv. 10–22).

B. *The Historicity of the Tabernacle.* That some kind of tent was used by the Hebrews as a centre of worship during the wanderings seems not unlikely (cf. xxxiii. 7–11) but such an elaborate structure as that described in P is hardly possible. Moreover it makes no appearance in those sources of the Pentateuch which are early, nor in the books of Samuel and Kings. It is only in Chronicles that the Tabernacle receives any adequate notice, and a comparison of the parallel passages such as 1 Kings iii. 4 ff. and 2 Chron. i. 3 ff. is very illuminating. Apart from its non-appearance in the earlier books the many discrepancies and difficulties in the description seem to suggest that an ideal and not an actual structure is being described; this however is not an argument that ought to be pressed as descriptions are often hard to follow and to understand for those who have not been eye-witnesses (cf. Caesar's bridge in *De Bell. Gall.* IV. 17). It is also a difficulty that so magnificent a tent should be produced by a collection of desert tribes recently escaped from bondage in Egypt. It is true that other passages refer to their possession of jewels and precious metal (xii. 35 f., xxxii. 2 ff.: cf. Jud. viii. 24 ff.) but the quantity pre-supposed by the requirements of xxxviii. 24 ff. is too great to be accounted for. Nor does it seem likely that they possessed the necessary skill, for even in Solomon's time it was found necessary to get a Tyrian workman to make the ornaments for the first temple (1 Kings vii. 13 ff.).

The simplest way of explaining the whole structure is to see in it a reading back of the glories of the temple into the first ages of the nation's history (cf. McNeile, pp. lxxxiii ff.).

7. THE HISTORY OF CONTEMPORARY EGYPT.

The sojourn of the Hebrew people in Egypt occupied practically the whole period covered by the eighteenth and nineteenth dynasties. If the tradition in xii. 40 can be accepted and if the people first came into Egypt 430 years before the Exodus they did so during the rule of the foreign dynasty known as the Hyksos or shepherd kings. These last were driven out in 1587 B.C. and a native dynasty established with Thebes as its headquarters. Under the kings of the eighteenth dynasty Egypt reached the very height of its power and influence. The greatest name amongst Egyptian sovereigns Thothmes III (1503–1449) belongs to it, and during his reign as a strong ruler he made repeated war on his neighbours, carrying the Egyptian arms even into Asia and being victorious in the famous battle of Megiddo. His immediate successors preserved the power of the kingdom at the same height, but under the famous "heretic" king Amenophis IV (1383–1365) internal dissensions began to shew themselves and a weakening of outward authority soon followed. The successor of Amenophis was his son-in-law Tutankhamen whose tomb has been recently discovered. His reign was the beginning of real decline and the dynasty which had begun with such splendour ended in 1328 with the prestige of the nation considerably lowered. The nineteenth dynasty (1328–1202) also made Thebes its capital and by the efforts of its earlier rulers did something to restore the military glory of Egypt. Seti I (1326–1300) drove back various Bedawin tribes and pushed north beyond Aleppo. His son and successor was Rameses II (1300–1234) perhaps the best known of all the Pharaohs, and the one who would be the chief disputant with Thothmes III for the foremost place amongst Egyptian rulers. Like his father he was a great conqueror though his struggles with the Hittites were perhaps not so successful as the Egyptians themselves represent. For our purposes however his building operations are more important, or more interesting, than his military exploits, for it must have been at his command that the Israelites were made to engage in the construction of the store cities of Raamses and Pithom (i. 11). Rameses II was thus the Pharaoh of the oppression. In addition to store cities and fortresses which he erected he also restored many temples, in his pride sometimes effacing the name of the original builder in order to insert his own.

Merenptah (1234-1214) followed his father, being probably nearly sixty years of age before the throne became his. The chief event of his reign was an attempted invasion by Libyan tribes and their allies from the Mediterranean coasts; they were defeated with great loss. To the student of Exodus however Merenptah is important as being in all probability the Pharaoh from whose rule the Hebrews made good their escape. The remaining years of the nineteenth dynasty (1214-1202) were a time of great weakness and internal disorder when the throne of Egypt was disputed by various claimants. At last Setnakht (1203-1202) succeeded in overcoming his rivals but did not live to enjoy his triumph. With his son Rameses III (1202-1171) begins the twentieth dynasty and a time of greater stability and better government. Rameses III like his great namesake was a builder and also a successful general. More than once he repelled invaders from the Egyptian dependencies in Canaan and Phoenicia but his most noteworthy exploit was the repulse of another attempt by the Libyans and their allies to enter Egypt; included amongst these invaders were the *Purasati* who are none other than the people known to us as the Philistines.

8. ANALYSIS.

A. i.–xiii. 16.   *The Israelites are rescued from bondage in Egypt.*

i.   The change in the attitude of the Egyptians towards Israel. The oppressive measures of Pharaoh.

ii. 1–22.   The birth of the deliverer, his adoption by Pharaoh's daughter, his flight to Midian.

ii. 23–iv. 17.   The call of Moses.

iv. 18–vi. 1.   Moses returns to Egypt, he and Aaron interview Pharaoh. The unfortunate consequences of their first efforts.

vi. 2–vii. 7.   Another account of the call of Moses.

vii. 8–xi.   The first nine plagues.

xii. 1–   The institution of the Passover. The
xiii. 16.   death of the firstborn. The flight from Egypt.

B. xiii. 17–xviii.   *The journeyings up to the arrival at Sinai.*

xiii. 17–   The passage of the Red Sea. The song
xv. 21.   of Moses.

xv. 22–27.   From the Red Sea to Elim.

xvi.   From Elim to the Wilderness of Sin. The quails and manna.

xvii. 1–7.   The strife at Massah and Meribah.

8–16.   The fight with Amalek.

xviii.   The visit of Jethro and the appointment of judges to assist Moses.

C. xix.–xl.   *Israel at Sinai.*

xix.   The arrival and the theophany.

xx.–xxiv.   The Decalogue and the Book of the Covenant.
xx. 1–21. The Decalogue.
xx. 22–xxiii. 33. The Book of the Covenant.
xxiv. 1–11. The vision of Jehovah.
xxiv. 12–18. Moses on the mount of God.

xxv.–xxxi.   The pattern of the tabernacle and of its furniture as given to Moses in the mount.

xxxii.   The Golden Calf.

xxxiii. 1–11. Jehovah refuses to go with the people. The tent of meeting.

xxxiii. 12–23. Moses sees the vision of God's glory.

xxxiv.   The renewal of the Covenant.

xxxv.–xl.   The carrying out of the commands given to Moses in the mount. The manufacture of the tabernacle and its furniture.

Note. The following passages are attributed to P by most scholars: i. 1–5, 7, 13 f., ii. 23 b–25, vi. 2–vii. 13, 19–20 a, 21 b–22, viii. 5–7, 15 b–19, ix. 8–12, xii. 1–20, 24, 28, 40–51, xiii. 1 f., 20, xiv. 1–4, 8 f., 15 b, 21 a, 21 c–23, 26, 28 f., xvi. (except 4 and 15), xvii. 1 a, xix. 1 f., xxiv. 15 a–18 a, xxv.–xxxi. 18 a, xxxiv. 29–xl.

THE SECOND BOOK OF MOSES,

COMMONLY CALLED

EXODUS

I—XIII. 16. The Deliverance from Egypt.

i. 1–7. *The sons of Jacob.*

Now these are the names of the sons of Israel, which 1
came into Egypt; every man and his household came with
Jacob. Reuben, Simeon, Levi, and Judah; Issachar, 2
Zebulun, and Benjamin; Dan and Naphtali, Gad and 4
Asher. And all the souls that came out of the loins of 5
Jacob were seventy souls: and Joseph was in Egypt
already. And Joseph died, and all his brethren, and all 6
that generation. And the children of Israel were fruitful, 7
and increased abundantly, and multiplied, and waxed exceeding mighty; and the land was filled with them.

---

i. 2–4. Notice that the sons of Israel are arranged, not in order
of birth, but according to their mothers: see Gen. xxxv. 23 ff.

5. seventy. The detailed list of names is to be found in Gen.
xlvi. 8–27. In the list in Numb. xxvi. five more of the descendants of Joseph are included making the full number 75. In the
passage in Gen. and here LXX accordingly has 75 souls, hence
the number in Acts vii. 14.

7. increased abundantly: lit. 'swarmed.' The word is not
generally used of men but of 'creeping things' as Gen. vii. 21;
Lev. xi. 29, etc. The Hebrews liked to emphasise the greatness
of the growth in Egypt: notice the fivefold description.

the land. Called Goshen according to J (Gen. xlvii. 4) or
Rameses according to P (Gen. xlvii. 11).

8-22. *The oppression of Israel.*

8 Now there arose a new king over Egypt, which knew
9 not Joseph. And he said unto his people, Behold, the
   people of the children of Israel are more and mightier
10 than we: come, let us deal wisely with them; lest they
   multiply, and it come to pass, that, when there falleth out
   any war, they also join themselves unto our enemies, and
11 fight against us, and get them up out of the land. Therefore they did set over them taskmasters to afflict them
   with their burdens. And they built for Pharaoh store cities,
12 Pithom and Raamses. But the more they afflicted them,
   the more they multiplied and the more they spread abroad.
   And they were grieved because of the children of Israel.
13 And the Egyptians made the children of Israel to serve
14 with rigour: and they made their lives bitter with hard

---

8. a new king. Probably Rameses II who is generally considered to be the Pharaoh of the oppression : see Introd. p. 16.

knew not Joseph. He took no account of his services and
therefore was not concerned to deal justly with his fellow-
countrymen.

10. deal wisely, i.e. 'craftily' (cf. Acts vii. 19 'subtilly').

our enemies. Perhaps the Hittites or more probably nomadic
tribes akin to the Hebrews themselves (see Introd. pp. 15 f.).
Egypt was readily invaded and Rameses II built forts to protect
the frontier.

11. to afflict them. Aristotle mentions compulsory labour as
a method adopted by tyrants for breaking the spirit of their subjects (*Politics*, VIII. (v) 11).

Pharaoh. Not a personal name but a title. The literal meaning
is 'great house' to which the phrase 'Sublime Porte' is often
quoted as a parallel.

Pithom. The site of this place was excavated by M. Naville in
1883 and inscriptions were found referring to Rameses II as the
founder. It is mentioned by Herodotus as Πάτουμος (II. 158).
Cf. further, Sayce, *The Egypt of the Hebs.* etc. pp. 43 f.

Raamses. The site of this city has not been definitely located.
Driver is inclined to favour *Tell er-Reṭābeh*, about 10 miles west
of Pithom, which was excavated by Flinders Petrie.

service, in mortar and in brick, and in all manner of
service in the field, all their service, wherein they made
them serve with rigour.

And the king of Egypt spake to the Hebrew mid- 15
wives, of which the name of the one was Shiphrah, and
the name of the other Puah : and he said, When ye do 16
the office of a midwife to the Hebrew women, and see
them upon the birthstool; if it be a son, then ye shall
kill him ; but if it be a daughter, then she shall live.
But the midwives feared God, and did not as the king of 17
Egypt commanded them, but saved the men children alive.
And the king of Egypt called for the midwives, and said 18
unto them, Why have ye done this thing, and have saved
the men children alive? And the midwives said unto 19
Pharaoh, Because the Hebrew women are not as the
Egyptian women ; for they are lively, and are delivered
ere the midwife come unto them. And God dealt well 20
with the midwives : and the people multiplied, and waxed
very mighty. And it came to pass, because the midwives 21
feared God, that he made them houses. And Pharaoh 22
charged all his people, saying, Every son that is born ye
shall cast into the river, and every daughter ye shall save
alive.

ii. 1–10. *The adoption of Moses.*

And there went a man of the house of Levi, and took **2**
to wife a daughter of Levi. And the woman conceived, 2

---

14. mortar. Lit. 'clay,' the black mud from the Nile.

the field. The Hebrews may have been employed as agricultural labourers, more probably they were engaged in irrigation
works. The Egyptians themselves left such operations to slaves
or captives.

21. houses. Not buildings but families: cf. Gen. xvi. 2
(marg.); 2 Sam. vii. 11 ; 1 Kings ii. 24.

ii. 1. a daughter of Levi. In Numb. xxvi. 59 rendered *the*
daughter of Levi. Her name was Jochebed.

and bare a son: and when she saw him that he was a
3 goodly child, she hid him three months. And when she
could not longer hide him, she took for him an ark of
bulrushes, and daubed it with slime and with pitch ; and
she put the child therein, and laid it in the flags by the
4 river's brink. And his sister stood afar off, to know what
5 would be done to him. And the daughter of Pharaoh came
down to bathe at the river; and her maidens walked along
by the river side ; and she saw the ark among the flags,
6 and sent her handmaid to fetch it. And she opened it,
and saw the child : and, behold, the babe wept. And she
had compassion on him, and said, This is one of the
7 Hebrews' children. Then said his sister to Pharaoh's
daughter, Shall I go and call thee a nurse of the Hebrew
8 women, that she may nurse the child for thee? And Pharaoh's
daughter said to her, Go. And the maid went and called
9 the child's mother. And Pharaoh's daughter said unto her,
Take this child away, and nurse it for me, and I will give
thee thy wages. And the woman took the child, and
10 nursed it. And the child grew, and she brought him unto

---

3. A number of instances of notable leaders who were exposed
in their infancy have been collected in Frazer, *Folk-Lore in O. T.*
II. pp. 438 ff. The most striking in its similarity is that of Sargon
of Akkad, who was left in a basket amongst the rushes of the
river.

an ark. The word is the same as that used for Noah's ark
(Gen. vi.–ix.) and is of Egyptian origin.

bulrushes. Cf. Isa. xviii. 2. The Egyptian custom of making
vessels of papyrus is referred to by Pliny, *Hist. Nat.* XIII. 22
and Lucan, *Phars.* IV. 136.

slime. That is 'bitumen': the object was to render the ark
watertight.

flags. Reeds : the same word is used in the 'Red' Sea, really
the Sea of Reeds (see note on xiii. 18).

5. the daughter of Pharaoh. Rameses II had 59 daughters.
The name of this one is given variously as Thermouthis (Josephus)
or Merris (Eusebius).

7. of the Hebrew women. A native woman would no doubt
have refused to nurse a foreign baby.

Pharaoh's daughter, and he became her son. And she called his name Moses, and said, Because I drew him out of the water.

11-22. *Moses in Midian.*

And it came to pass in those days, when Moses was 11 grown up, that he went out unto his brethren, and looked on their burdens: and he saw an Egyptian smiting an Hebrew, one of his brethren. And he looked this 12 way and that way, and when he saw that there was no man, he smote the Egyptian, and hid him in the sand. And he went out the second day, and, behold, two men 13 of the Hebrews strove together : and he said to him that did the wrong, Wherefore smitest thou thy fellow? And he 14 said, Who made thee a prince and a judge over us? thinkest thou to kill me, as thou killedst the Egyptian? And Moses feared, and said, Surely the thing is known. Now when Pharaoh heard this thing, he sought to slay 15 Moses. But Moses fled from the face of Pharaoh, and dwelt in the land of Midian : and he sat down by a well.

---

10. became her son. Cf. Acts vii. 22; Heb. xi. 24.

Moses. Heb. *Mōsheh.* Probably derived from the Egyptian *mosi* = 'born' as in the case of the great Egyptian ruler Thothmes which should be read Thutmosi. The explanation given in the text depending as it does upon a Hebrew root is hardly likely to have occurred to an Egyptian princess, nor is it grammatically possible.

11. was grown up. A considerable interval must have elapsed, nearly 40 years, according to Acts vii. 23.

looked on. The reply in *v.* 14 may have been partly inspired by ill-feeling towards Moses because of his more fortunate fate.

14. a prince and a judge. Moses' lack of authority is pointed out.

15. Moses fled. As did Jacob (Gen. xxvii. 43), David (1 Sam. xix. 12), and Elijah (1 Kings xix. 3) before persecution.

Midian. To the east of Canaan. The Midianites, like the Hebrews, claimed descent from Abraham, but by a different wife.

16 Now the priest of Midian had seven daughters: and they
came and drew water, and filled the troughs to water their
17 father's flock. And the shepherds came and drove them
away: but Moses stood up and helped them, and watered
18 their flock. And when they came to Reuel their father, he
19 said, How is it that ye are come so soon to-day? And
they said, An Egyptian delivered us out of the hand of the
shepherds, and moreover he drew water for us, and
20 watered the flock. And he said unto his daughters, And
where is he? why is it that ye have left the man? call him,
21 that he may eat bread. And Moses was content to dwell
with the man: and he gave Moses Zipporah his daughter.
22 And she bare a son, and he called his name Gershom:
for he said, I have been a sojourner in a strange land.

23–25. God takes notice of the oppression of Israel.

23 And it came to pass in the course of those many days,
that the king of Egypt died: and the children of Israel
sighed by reason of the bondage, and they cried, and their
24 cry came up unto God by reason of the bondage. And

16. the priest of Midian. This will mean not the *only* priest
of the Midianites but the *chief* one.

daughters. It must not be supposed that poverty or a humble
situation was the cause of this service (cf. Gen. xxix. 1–6). Even
in the present day the flocks of the Bedawin are often cared for
by the unmarried women of the tribe: see Frazer, *Folk-Lore in
O.T.* II. pp. 81 ff.

18. Reuel. Called Jethro in E (iii. 1, xviii. 1, etc.). It is
possible that he had two names. In the original of Jud. i. 16,
iv. 11 he is called Hobab.

19. An Egyptian. Moses was doubtless still clad as an Egyptian
noble.

22. Gershom. The name is explained by a pun: cf. *v.* 10.
LXX adds a second son Eliezer (cf. xviii. 3).

strange, i.e. 'foreign.'

23. the king of Egypt died. Moses would thus be able to
return: cf. iv. 19 and Matt. ii. 19 f. where the death of Herod
enabled the infant Saviour to return to Palestine.

God heard their groaning, and God remembered his covenant with Abraham, with Isaac, and with Jacob. And 25
God saw the children of Israel, and God took knowledge
of them.

iii. *The call of Moses.*

Now Moses was keeping the flock of Jethro his father 3
in law, the priest of Midian: and he led the flock to
the back of the wilderness, and came to the mountain
of God, unto Horeb. And the angel of the LORD appeared 2
unto him in a flame of fire out of the midst of a bush: and
he looked, and, behold, the bush burned with fire, and the
bush was not consumed. And Moses said, I will turn aside 3
now, and see this great sight, why the bush is not burnt.
And when the LORD saw that he turned aside to see, God 4
called unto him out of the midst of the bush, and said,
Moses, Moses. And he said, Here am I. And he said, 5
Draw not nigh hither: put off thy shoes from off thy feet,
for the place whereon thou standest is holy ground.

---

iii. 1. Horeb. The name used in E and D instead of the more
usual Sinai of J and P. Possibly the two names have not an
identical reference, Horeb may be a wider term including Sinai
within it.

2. the angel of the LORD. When LORD is printed in capitals
it represents the divine personal name generally rendered Jehovah. This word is not the original Hebrew but is made up of a
combination of the consonants of the personal name (jhwh) with
the vowels of the Hebrew for Lord, which in reading was substituted for it. The exact form of the name of the God of Israel
has been lost, though it was probably Jahweh. The angel was
really a manifestation of God Himself.

a flame of fire. The divine presence is often revealed by fire
(e.g. xix. 18; Ezek. i. 27, viii. 2); cf. Homer, *Od.* XIX. 39 f.

a bush: a bramble, *Rubus fruticosus.*

4. the LORD...God. The use of different words to represent
the deity suggests the use of different sources.

shoes, i.e. 'sandals.' To remove the sandals on entering a
mosque or holy place is still customary in the East.

6 Moreover he said, I am the God of thy father, the God of Abraham, the God of Isaac, and the God of Jacob. And Moses hid his face; for he was afraid to look upon
7 God. And the LORD said, I have surely seen the affliction of my people which are in Egypt, and have heard their cry by reason of their taskmasters; for I
8 know their sorrows; and I am come down to deliver them out of the hand of the Egyptians, and to bring them up out of that land unto a good land and a large, unto a land flowing with milk and honey; unto the place of the Canaanite, and the Hittite, and the Amorite, and the
9 Perizzite, and the Hivite, and the Jebusite. And now, behold, the cry of the children of Israel is come unto me: moreover I have seen the oppression wherewith the

---

6. I am the God, etc. God is the God of the living and the patriarchs still live in Him (Mk. xii. 26 and parallels). Moses was not to go to the people in the name of a strange or unknown deity.

8. am come down. So xix. 11, 18, 20; Gen. xi. 5, 7 (all J). God is represented as needing to come down to find out the conditions.

a land flowing, etc. A common expression in J and D; found outside the Pentateuch in Josh. v. 6; Jer. xi. 5, xxxii. 22; Ezek. xx. 6, 15.

honey probably included various fruit syrups.

the Canaanite. The term is used of the dwellers in Canaan in general but more particularly of those living in the lowlands, on the coast, and in the Jordan valley (Numb. xiii. 29).

the Hittite. This people once ruled a great empire with capitals in Asia Minor and at Carchemish. The reference here is perhaps to scattered bodies left behind when the nation as a whole had withdrawn northwards.

the Amorite. Used of the people of Canaan by E and D, and in particular of those living in the hill-country. This seems to distinguish them from the Canaanites, just as the Scots were distinguished from the Picts who dwelt in the plains.

the Perizzite, and the Hivite. These people of whom nothing else is known lived in Central Palestine. The former word may be an equivalent for peasant and so not a race name at all.

the Jebusite. The people of Jerusalem, afterwards conquered by David.

Egyptians oppress them. Come now therefore, and I will 10
send thee unto Pharaoh, that thou mayest bring forth my
people the children of Israel out of Egypt. And Moses 11
said unto God, Who am I, that I should go unto Pharaoh,
and that I should bring forth the children of Israel out of
Egypt? And he said, Certainly I will be with thee; and 12
this shall be the token unto thee, that I have sent thee:
when thou hast brought forth the people out of Egypt, ye shall
serve God upon this mountain. And Moses said unto God, 13
Behold, when I come unto the children of Israel, and shall
say unto them, The God of your fathers hath sent me unto
you; and they shall say to me, What is his name? what shall
I say unto them? And God said unto Moses, I AM THAT I 14
AM: and he said, Thus shalt thou say unto the children
of Israel, I AM hath sent me unto you. And God said 15
moreover unto Moses, Thus shalt thou say unto the
children of Israel, The LORD, the God of your fathers,
the God of Abraham, the God of Isaac, and the God of
Jacob, hath sent me unto you: this is my name for ever,
and this is my memorial unto all generations. Go, and 16
gather the elders of Israel together, and say unto them,
The LORD, the God of your fathers, the God of Abraham,
of Isaac, and of Jacob, hath appeared unto me, saying, I
have surely visited you, and *seen* that which is done to
you in Egypt: and I have said, I will bring you up out of 17
the affliction of Egypt unto the land of the Canaanite, and

---

11. Who am I? Moses thinks only of his own powers and
forgets the divine strength.
14. I AM THAT I AM. Driver prefers ' I will be that I will be.'
The name represents the character of Jahweh which will be revealed more and more in the history of His people. (See Introd.
p. 8 and notes in McNeile, pp. 21 ff.; Driver, p. 40).
16. the elders. The older men to whom authority was given.
In primitive peoples this was a usual form of government: cf. the
Anglo-Saxon 'Alderman' (a name which is still retained in
municipal life), the Roman 'Patres' and 'Senatus.'
17. Canaanite, etc. See on *v.* 8.

the Hittite, and the Amorite, and the Perizzite, and the
Hivite, and the Jebusite, unto a land flowing with milk
18 and honey. And they shall hearken to thy voice : and
thou shalt come, thou and the elders of Israel, unto the
king of Egypt, and ye shall say unto him, The LORD, the
God of the Hebrews, hath met with us : and now let us
go, we pray thee, three days' journey into the wilderness,
19 that we may sacrifice to the LORD our God. And I know
that the king of Egypt will not give you leave to go, no,
20 not by a mighty hand. And I will put forth my hand, and
smite Egypt with all my wonders which I will do in the
21 midst thereof : and after that he will let you go. And I
will give this people favour in the sight of the Egyptians :
and it shall come to pass, that, when ye go, ye shall not go
22 empty : but every woman shall ask of her neighbour, and
of her that sojourneth in her house, jewels of silver, and
jewels of gold, and raiment : and ye shall put them upon
your sons, and upon your daughters ; and ye shall spoil
the Egyptians.

iv. 1–17. *God re-assures Moses by signs and promises.*

4 And Moses answered and said, But, behold, they will
not believe me, nor hearken unto my voice : for they will
2 say, The LORD hath not appeared unto thee. And the
LORD said unto him, What is that in thine hand ? And
3 he said, A rod. And he said, Cast it on the ground. And
he cast it on the ground, and it became a serpent ; and
4 Moses fled from before it. And the LORD said unto Moses,

---

18. three days'…sacrifice. Not to Sinai which was much too
far. Perhaps the request was merely an excuse for getting away
from Egypt (cf. vi. 11, x. 9 f.). ·

22. her neighbour. E regards the people as living amongst
the Egyptians (cf. viii. 22).

that sojourneth. Maidservants or slaves presumably; cf. Job
xix. 15.

iv. 2. rod. His shepherd's staff.

Put forth thine hand, and take it by the tail: (and he put forth his hand, and laid hold of it, and it became a rod in his hand:) that they may believe that the LORD, the God 5 of their fathers, the God of Abraham, the God of Isaac, and the God of Jacob, hath appeared unto thee. And the 6 LORD said furthermore unto him, Put now thine hand into thy bosom. And he put his hand into his bosom: and when he took it out, behold, his hand was leprous, as *white as* snow. And he said, Put thine hand into thy 7 bosom again. (And he put his hand into his bosom again; and when he took it out of his bosom, behold, it was turned again as his *other* flesh.) And it shall come to pass, 8 if they will not believe thee, neither hearken to the voice of the first sign, that they will believe the voice of the latter sign. And it shall come to pass, if they will not 9 believe even these two signs, neither hearken unto thy voice, that thou shalt take of the water of the river, and pour it upon the dry land : and the water which thou takest out of the river shall become blood upon the dry land. And Moses said unto the LORD, Oh Lord, I am 10 not eloquent, neither heretofore, nor since thou hast spoken unto thy servant : for I am slow of speech, and of a slow tongue. And the LORD said unto him, Who hath 11 made man's mouth ? or who maketh *a man* dumb, or deaf, or seeing, or blind ? is it not I the LORD ? Now therefore 12 go, and I will be with thy mouth, and teach thee what thou shalt speak. And he said, O Lord, send, I pray 13 thee, by the hand of him whom thou wilt send. And the 14 anger of the LORD was kindled against Moses, and he said,

---

6. thy bosom. The fold of the garment; so Ps. lxxiv. 11.
snow. So of Miriam (Numb. xii. 10) and Gehazi (2 Kings v. 27).
9. water...blood. Cf. the first plague (vii. 14-25).
13. him whom, etc. Moses makes an ungracious submission.

Is there not Aaron thy brother the Levite? I know that
he can speak well. And also, behold, he cometh forth to
meet thee : and when he seeth thee, he will be glad in his
15 heart. And thou shalt speak unto him, and put the words
in his mouth : and I will be with thy mouth, and with his
16 mouth, and will teach you what ye shall do. And he shall
be thy spokesman unto the people : and it shall come to
pass, that he shall be to thee a mouth, and thou shalt be to
17 him as God. And thou shalt take in thine hand this rod,
wherewith thou shalt do the signs.

18-26. *Moses returns to Egypt.*

18 And Moses went and returned to Jethro his father in
law, and said unto him, Let me go, I pray thee, and return
unto my brethren which are in Egypt, and see whether
they be yet alive. And Jethro said to Moses, Go in peace.
19 And the LORD said unto Moses in Midian, Go, return into
Egypt: for all the men are dead which sought thy life.
20 And Moses took his wife and his sons, and set them upon
an ass, and he returned to the land of Egypt: and Moses
21 took the rod of God in his hand. And the LORD said unto
Moses, When thou goest back into Egypt, see that thou
do before Pharaoh all the wonders which I have put in
thine hand : but I will harden his heart, and he will not
22 let the people go. And thou shalt say unto Pharaoh, Thus

---

14. the Levite. Levite is used here of a profession (= clergy-
man), not of membership of a tribe: Moses himself was a Levite
by birth.

16. as God. Inspiring his words: cf. Aeschylus, *Eum.* 17 f.
So in vii. 1 (P) Moses is made a god to Pharaoh. This exaltation
of Moses finds expression in the story of Numb. xii. 1 ff.

17. this rod. A different rod it would seem from that in *v.* 2 ;
cf. *v.* 20.

19. This *v.* seems to be out of its context.

20. sons. This should be singular : see ii. 22, iv. 22.

saith the LORD, Israel is my son, my firstborn: and I have 23
said unto thee, Let my son go, that he may serve me;
and thou hast refused to let him go: behold, I will slay
thy son, thy firstborn. And it came to pass on the way at 24
the lodging place, that the LORD met him, and sought to
kill him. Then Zipporah took a flint, and cut off the fore- 25
skin of her son, and cast it at his feet; and she said, Surely
a bridegroom of blood art thou to me. So he let him 26
alone. Then she said, A bridegroom of blood *art thou*,
because of the circumcision.

27–31. *Moses and Aaron are accepted by the people.*

And the LORD said to Aaron, Go into the wilderness to 27
meet Moses. And he went, and met him in the mountain
of God, and kissed him. And Moses told Aaron all the 28
words of the LORD wherewith he had sent him, and all
the signs wherewith he had charged him. And Moses and 29
Aaron went and gathered together all the elders of the
children of Israel: and Aaron spake all the words which 30
the LORD had spoken unto Moses, and did the signs in
the sight of the people. And the people believed: and 31
when they heard that the LORD had visited the children
of Israel, and that he had seen their affliction, then they
bowed their heads and worshipped.

v. 1-vi. 1. *Pharaoh rejects the message of God and
increases the burdens of the Israelites.*

And afterwards Moses and Aaron came, and said unto 5
Pharaoh, Thus saith the LORD, the God of Israel, Let my

---

22. my firstborn. The nation is God's son, the object of His
love; cf. Hos. xi. 1 and Jer. xxxi. 9 with the present writer's note.
24. sought to kill him. Probably a sudden illness befell Moses.
25. a flint. Either a reminiscence of an older age when metal
was not used, or an archaism in connexion with a ritual act.
his feet. A euphemism as in Isa. vii. 20.
bridegroom of blood. The circumcision of the son was taken
in place of that of the father. It is possible that a Hebrew was
circumcised before marriage: see Driver, p. 33.

people go, that they may hold a feast unto me in the
2 wilderness. And Pharaoh said, Who is the LORD, that I
should hearken unto his voice to let Israel go? I know
not the LORD, and moreover I will not let Israel go.
3 And they said, The God of the Hebrews hath met
with us : let us go, we pray thee, three days' journey
into the wilderness, and sacrifice unto the LORD our
God; lest he fall upon us with pestilence, or with the
4 sword. And the king of Egypt said unto them, Wherefore
do ye, Moses and Aaron, loose the people from their works?
5 get you unto your burdens. And Pharaoh said, Behold, the
people of the land are now many, and ye make them rest
6 from their burdens. And the same day Pharaoh commanded the taskmasters of the people, and their officers,
7 saying, Ye shall no more give the people straw to make
brick, as heretofore: let them go and gather straw for them-
8 selves. And the tale of the bricks, which they did make
heretofore, ye shall lay upon them; ye shall not diminish
aught thereof: for they be idle; therefore they cry, saying,
9 Let us go and sacrifice to our God. Let heavier work be
laid upon the men, that they may labour therein; and let
10 them not regard lying words. And the taskmasters of the
people went out, and their officers, and they spake to the
people, saying, Thus saith Pharaoh, I will not give you

---

v. 1. a feast. Better a 'pilgrimage' (Heb. *ḥag*=Arab. *haj*,
used of the pilgrimage to Mecca).
5. the people of the land. Used in the more obvious sense
of natives in Gen. xxiii. 7. Later it came to mean the common-
alty, the crowd, or even the laity in contrast with the Levites
(Zech. vii. 5).
6. taskmasters...officers. The Egyptian managers and the
Hebrew 'foremen' subordinate to them.
7. The bricks were made from the mud of the Nile sometimes
mixed with chopped straw or stubble: see description and illustration in Driver, pp. 37 ff.
8. tale, i.e. 'fixed amount,' 'quota.'

straw. Go yourselves, get you straw where ye can find it: 11
for nought of your work shall be diminished. So the people 12
were scattered abroad throughout all the land of Egypt to
gather stubble for straw. And the taskmasters were urgent, 13
saying, Fulfil your works, *your* daily tasks, as when there
was straw. And the officers of the children of Israel, which 14
Pharaoh's taskmasters had set over them, were beaten,
and demanded, Wherefore have ye not fulfilled your task
both yesterday and to-day, in making brick as heretofore?
Then the officers of the children of Israel came and cried 15
unto Pharaoh, saying, Wherefore dealest thou thus with
thy servants? There is no straw given unto thy servants, 16
and they say to us, Make brick: and, behold, thy servants
are beaten; but the fault is in thine own people. But he 17
said, Ye are idle, ye are idle: therefore ye say, Let us go
and sacrifice to the LORD. Go therefore now, and work; 18
for there shall no straw be given you, yet shall ye deliver
the tale of bricks. And the officers of the children of Israel 19
did see that they were in evil case, when it was said, Ye
shall not minish aught from your bricks, *your* daily tasks,
And they met Moses and Aaron, who stood in the way, as 20
they came forth from Pharaoh: and they said unto them, 21
The LORD look upon you, and judge; because ye have
made our savour to be abhorred in the eyes of Pharaoh,
and in the eyes of his servants, to put a sword in their hand
to slay us. And Moses returned unto the LORD, and said, 22
Lord, wherefore hast thou evil entreated this people? why
is it that thou hast sent me? For since I came to Pharaoh 23
to speak in thy name, he hath evil entreated this people;

---

16. the fault is in thine own people. Heb. is corrupt. LXX
renders 'thou sinnest against thine own people.' That a people
should be willing, when it suited their purpose, to acknowledge
a rule which they hated is in accordance with history (cf. John
xix. 15).

21. savour to be abhorred, i.e. 'brought us into bad odour.'

6 neither hast thou delivered thy people at all. And the
  LORD said unto Moses, Now shalt thou see what I will
  do to Pharaoh : for by a strong hand shall he let them go,
  and by a strong hand shall he drive them out of his land.

vi. 2–13. *Another account of the call.*

2   And God spake unto Moses, and said unto him, I am
3 JEHOVAH : and I appeared unto Abraham, unto Isaac, and
  unto Jacob, as God Almighty, but by my name JEHOVAH
4 I was not known to them. And I have also established my
  covenant with them, to give them the land of Canaan, the
5 land of their sojournings, wherein they sojourned. And
  moreover I have heard the groaning of the children of
  Israel, whom the Egyptians keep in bondage ; and I have
6 remembered my covenant. Wherefore say unto the children
  of Israel, I am Jehovah, and I will bring you out from
  under the burdens of the Egyptians, and I will rid you out
  of their bondage, and I will redeem you with a stretched
7 out arm, and with great judgements : and I will take you
  to me for a people, and I will be to you a God : and ye
  shall know that I am Jehovah your God, which bringeth
8 you out from under the burdens of the Egyptians. And I

---

vi. 3. God Almighty. Heb. *El Shaddai.* The exact meaning
of Shaddai is not known ; the Heb. root = to destroy, but such
a meaning does not suit the contexts (Gen. xvii. 1, xxviii. 3,
xxxv. 11, etc.) in which it occurs. The Assyrian *Shadū* = 'mountain' suggests a possible interpretation especially when proper
names like Bel-shadūa (i.e. Bel is my mountain) are taken into
account (see McNeile, pp. 40 f).

not known. As the earlier parts of the Pentateuch are full of
the name Jehovah we have here an instance of the use of a different source : P avoids using Jehovah before this point.

4. established. P never speaks of 'cutting' a covenant which
is the usual Heb. expression.

6. redeem. Heb. *gā'al* almost = vindicate, reclaim. There is
no idea of making a payment to anyone.

will bring you in unto the land, concerning which I lifted
up my hand to give it to Abraham, to Isaac, and to Jacob;
and I will give it you for an heritage: I am Jehovah.
And Moses spake so unto the children of Israel: but they 9
hearkened not unto Moses for anguish of spirit, and for
cruel bondage.

And the LORD spake unto Moses, saying, Go in, speak $^{10}_{11}$
unto Pharaoh king of Egypt, that he let the children of
Israel go out of his land. And Moses spake before the 12
LORD, saying, Behold, the children of Israel have not
hearkened unto me; how then shall Pharaoh hear me, who
am of uncircumcised lips? And the LORD spake unto 13
Moses and unto Aaron, and gave them a charge unto the
children of Israel, and unto Pharaoh king of Egypt, to
bring the children of Israel out of the land of Egypt.

14-27. *The elders of Israel.*

These are the heads of their fathers' houses: the sons 14
of Reuben the firstborn of Israel; Hanoch, and Pallu,
Hezron, and Carmi: these are the families of Reuben.
And the sons of Simeon; Jemuel, and Jamin, and Ohad, 15
and Jachin, and Zohar, and Shaul the son of a Canaanitish
woman: these are the families of Simeon. And these are 16
the names of the sons of Levi according to their generations; Gershon, and Kohath, and Merari: and the years
of the life of Levi were an hundred thirty and seven years.
The sons of Gershon; Libni and Shimei, according to 17
their families. And the sons of Kohath; Amram, and Iz- 18
har, and Hebron, and Uzziel: and the years of the life of
Kohath were an hundred thirty and three years. And the 19
sons of Merari; Mahli and Mushi. These are the families

---

8. lifted up. In taking an oath: xvii. 26, etc.; cf. Virgil, *Aen.*
XII. 196.

12. uncircumcised lips. The expression is applied to ears
in Jer. vi. 10, and implies a lack of readiness.

20 of the Levites according to their generations. And Amram
took him Jochebed his father's sister to wife; and she bare
him Aaron and Moses: and the years of the life of Amram
21 were an hundred and thirty and seven years. And the
22 sons of Izhar; Korah, and Nepheg, and Zichri. And the
23 sons of Uzziel; Mishael, and Elzaphan, and Sithri. And
Aaron took him Elisheba, the daughter of Amminadab,
the sister of Nahshon, to wife; and she bare him Nadab
24 and Abihu, Eleazar and Ithamar. And the sons of Korah;
Assir, and Elkanah, and Abiasaph; these are the families
25 of the Korahites. And Eleazar Aaron's son took him one
of the daughters of Putiel to wife; and she bare him
Phinehas. These are the heads of the fathers' *houses* of
26 the Levites according to their families. These are that
Aaron and Moses, to whom the LORD said, Bring out the
children of Israel from the land of Egypt according to
27 their hosts. These are they which spake to Pharaoh king
of Egypt, to bring out the children of Israel from Egypt:
these are that Moses and Aaron.

vi. 28-vii. 7. *Threats against Egypt.*

28   And it came to pass on the day when the LORD spake
29 unto Moses in the land of Egypt, that the LORD spake
unto Moses, saying, I am the LORD: speak thou unto
30 Pharaoh king of Egypt all that I speak unto thee. And
Moses said before the LORD, Behold, I am of uncircum-

---

20. his father's sister. Such a union is regarded by Lev.
xviii. 12 as incestuous; this may have been an additional reason
for the exposure of Moses: cf. Frazer, *Folk-Lore, etc.* II. p. 454.
23. Nahshon. An ancestor of our Lord (Matt. i. 4).
Nadab, etc. See on xxiv. 1, xxviii. 1.
25. Putiel. An Egyptian name with *El* added. Nothing
more is known of him.
Phinehas. An Egyptian name = the negro. Phinehas played a
great part in P's story of the wanderings: see Numb. xxv. 7 ff.,
xxxi. 6, etc.

cised lips, and how shall Pharaoh hearken unto me? And **7**
the LORD said unto Moses, See, I have made thee a god
to Pharaoh : and Aaron thy brother shall be thy prophet.
Thou shalt speak all that I command thee: and Aaron thy **2**
brother shall speak unto Pharaoh, that he let the children of
Israel go out of his land. And I will harden Pharaoh's **3**
heart, and multiply my signs and my wonders in the land
of Egypt. But Pharaoh will not hearken unto you, and I **4**
will lay my hand upon Egypt, and bring forth my hosts,
my people the children of Israel, out of the land of Egypt
by great judgements. And the Egyptians shall know that **5**
I am the LORD, when I stretch forth mine hand upon
Egypt, and bring out the children of Israel from among
them. And Moses and Aaron did so; as the LORD com- **6**
manded them, so did they. And Moses was fourscore years **7**
old, and Aaron fourscore and three years old, when they
spake unto Pharaoh.

vii. 8–13. *Aaron's rod becomes a serpent.*

And the LORD spake unto Moses and unto Aaron, saying, **8**
When Pharaoh shall speak unto you, saying, Shew a **9**
wonder for you : then thou shalt say unto Aaron, Take
thy rod, and cast it down before Pharaoh, that it become
a serpent. And Moses and Aaron went in unto Pharaoh, **10**
and they did so, as the LORD had commanded : and Aaron
cast down his rod before Pharaoh and before his servants,
and it became a serpent. Then Pharaoh also called for **11**
the wise men and the sorcerers : and they also, the magicians of Egypt, did in like manner with their enchantments.

---

vii. 1. a god. Cf. iv. 16 (JE) with note.
6. did so. The details are contained in *vv.* 8 ff.
9. thy rod. In P belonging to Aaron.
serpent. Heb. *tannin,* i.e. 'reptile' (?young crocodile); cf. iv. 13.
11. magicians. Jannes and Jambres by name, according to
tradition (cf. 2 Tim. iii. 8). The practice of magic was common
in Egypt ; cf. Gen. xli. 8.

12 For they cast down every man his rod, and they became
13 serpents : but Aaron's rod swallowed up their rods. And
Pharaoh's heart was hardened, and he hearkened not unto
them; as the LORD had spoken.

14-25. (1) *The water turned to blood.*

14   And the LORD said unto Moses, Pharaoh's heart is
15 stubborn, he refuseth to let the people go. Get thee unto
Pharaoh in the morning ; lo, he goeth out unto the water;
and thou shalt stand by the river's brink to meet him ; and
the rod which was turned to a serpent shalt thou take in
16 thine hand. And thou shalt say unto him, The LORD, the
God of the Hebrews, hath sent me unto thee, saying, Let
my people go, that they may serve me in the wilderness:
17 and, behold, hitherto thou hast not hearkened. Thus saith
the LORD, In this thou shalt know that I am the LORD:
behold, I will smite with the rod that is in mine hand upon
the waters which are in the river, and they shall be turned
18 to blood. And the fish that is in the river shall die, and
the river shall stink ; and the Egyptians shall loathe to
19 drink water from the river. And the LORD said unto
Moses, Say unto Aaron, Take thy rod, and stretch out
thine hand over the waters of Egypt, over their rivers,
over their streams, and over their pools, and over all their

---

13. was hardened. God only 'hardens those who begin by hardening themselves' (Driver).

14 ff. In this plague, as in most of the others, a natural basis can be found for the story. The miracle consists in the unaccustomed severity of the visitation and the opportune moment of its occurrence.

17. to blood. 'When the Nile first begins to rise...the red marl brought from the mountains of Abyssinia stains it to a dark colour, which glistens like blood in the light of the setting sun' (Sayce).

18. fish. A principal article of diet: cf. Numb. xi. 5.

19. the waters, etc. P heightens the effect of the miracle by applying it not to the Nile only but to all the water.

ponds of water, that they may become blood; and there
shall be blood throughout all the land of Egypt, both in
vessels of wood and in vessels of stone. And Moses and 20
Aaron did so, as the LORD commanded; and he lifted up
the rod, and smote the waters that were in the river, in
the sight of Pharaoh, and in the sight of his servants; and
all the waters that were in the river were turned to blood.
And the fish that was in the river died; and the river stank, 21
and the Egyptians could not drink water from the river;
and the blood was throughout all the land of Egypt. And 22
the magicians of Egypt did in like manner with their enchantments: and Pharaoh's heart was hardened, and he
hearkened not unto them; as the LORD had spoken. And 23
Pharaoh turned and went into his house, neither did he
lay even this to heart. And all the Egyptians digged round 24
about the river for water to drink; for they could not drink
of the water of the river. And seven days were fulfilled, 25
after that the LORD had smitten the river.

viii. 1–15. (2) *The plague of frogs.*

And the LORD spake unto Moses, Go in unto Pharaoh, 8
and say unto him, Thus saith the LORD, Let my people
go, that they may serve me. And if thou refuse to let them 2
go, behold, I will smite all thy borders with frogs: and the 3
river shall swarm with frogs, which shall go up and come
into thine house, and into thy bedchamber, and upon thy
bed, and into the house of thy servants, and upon thy
people, and into thine ovens, and into thy kneadingtroughs:
and the frogs shall come up both upon thee, and upon thy 4

---

viii. 2. frogs. Not mentioned in O.T. except in connexion
with this plague. Similar plagues are described by Pliny and
other ancient writers.

3. ovens, i.e. portable earthenware stoves.

kneadingtroughs: better 'kneading-bowls,' such as are still
in use.

5 people, and upon all thy servants. And the LORD said
unto Moses, Say unto Aaron, Stretch forth thine hand with
thy rod over the rivers, over the streams, and over the
pools, and cause frogs to come up upon the land of Egypt.
6 And Aaron stretched out his hand over the waters of
Egypt; and the frogs came up, and covered the land of
7 Egypt. And the magicians did in like manner with their
enchantments, and brought up frogs upon the land of
8 Egypt. Then Pharaoh called for Moses and Aaron, and
said, Intreat the LORD, that he take away the frogs from
me, and from my people; and I will let the people go, that
9 they may sacrifice unto the LORD. And Moses said unto
Pharaoh, Have thou this glory over me: against what time
shall I intreat for thee, and for thy servants, and for thy
people, that the frogs be destroyed from thee and thy houses,
10 and remain in the river only? And he said, Against to-
morrow. And he said, Be it according to thy word: that
thou mayest know that there is none like unto the LORD
11 our God. And the frogs shall depart from thee, and from
thy houses, and from thy servants, and from thy people;
12 they shall remain in the river only. And Moses and Aaron
went out from Pharaoh: and Moses cried unto the LORD
concerning the frogs which he had brought upon Pharaoh.
13 And the LORD did according to the word of Moses; and
the frogs died out of the houses, out of the courts, and out
14 of the fields. And they gathered them together in heaps:
15 and the land stank. But when Pharaoh saw that there was
respite, he hardened his heart, and hearkened not unto
them; as the LORD had spoken.

---

7. the magicians apparently add to the woes of their fellows
instead of abating them.

9. Have thou, etc.: lit. 'Glorify thyself,' i.e. by fixing your
own time for the plague to cease. Similar expressions are used
of God (Isa. xliv. 23, etc.) and also of men vaunting themselves
(Jud. vii. 2).

16–19. (3) *The plague of lice.*

And the LORD said unto Moses, Say unto Aaron, Stretch 16
out thy rod, and smite the dust of the earth, that it may
become lice throughout all the land of Egypt. And they 17
did so; and Aaron stretched out his hand with his rod,
and smote the dust of the earth, and there were lice upon
man, and upon beast; all the dust of the earth became
lice throughout all the land of Egypt. And the magicians 18
did so with their enchantments to bring forth lice, but they
could not: and there were lice upon man, and upon beast.
Then the magicians said unto Pharaoh, This is the finger 19
of God: and Pharaoh's heart was hardened, and he hearkened not unto them; as the LORD had spoken.

20–32. (4) *The plague of flies.*

And the LORD said unto Moses, Rise up early in the 20
morning, and stand before Pharaoh; lo, he cometh forth
to the water; and say unto him, Thus saith the LORD,
Let my people go, that they may serve me. Else, if thou 21
wilt not let my people go, behold, I will send swarms of
flies upon thee, and upon thy servants, and upon thy people,
and into thy houses: and the houses of the Egyptians
shall be full of swarms of flies, and also the ground whereon
they are. And I will sever in that day the land of Goshen, 22
in which my people dwell, that no swarms of flies shall be

---

16. lice, better 'mosquitoes' (LXX σκνῖφες) : cf. Herodotus
II. 95.
19. the finger of God : cf. Luke xi. 20.
21. flies. Probably the dog-fly. Flies seem to have been a
common feature in Egypt (cf. Isa. vii. 18).
22. will sever. Swarms of flies come up with the wind and
sometimes do not affect certain districts.
Goshen. Probably about forty miles N.E. of Cairo round *Kes*
(the modern Saft-el Ḥenna): the district covers about seventy
square miles.
my people dwell. J pictures the Israelites living apart: cf. iii.
22 (E). Perhaps they had the country allotted to them whilst
the Egyptians occupied the town.

there; to the end thou mayest know that I am the LORD
23 in the midst of the earth. And I will put a division between
my people and thy people: by to-morrow shall this sign
24 be. And the LORD did so; and there came grievous swarms
of flies into the house of Pharaoh, and into his servants'
houses: and in all the land of Egypt the land was corrupted
25 by reason of the swarms of flies. And Pharaoh called for
Moses and for Aaron, and said, Go ye, sacrifice to your
26 God in the land. And Moses said, It is not meet so to do;
for we shall sacrifice the abomination of the Egyptians to
the LORD our God: lo, shall we sacrifice the abomination
of the Egyptians before their eyes, and will they not stone
27 us? We will go three days' journey into the wilderness,
and sacrifice to the LORD our God, as he shall command
28 us. And Pharaoh said, I will let you go, that ye may
sacrifice to the LORD your God in the wilderness; only ye
29 shall not go very far away: intreat for me. And Moses
said, Behold, I go out from thee, and I will intreat the
LORD that the swarms of flies may depart from Pharaoh,
from his servants, and from his people, to-morrow: only
let not Pharaoh deal deceitfully any more in not letting
30 the people go to sacrifice to the LORD. And Moses went
31 out from Pharaoh, and intreated the LORD. And the LORD
did according to the word of Moses; and he removed the
swarms of flies from Pharaoh, from his servants, and from
32 his people; there remained not one. And Pharaoh hardened his heart this time also, and he did not let the people
go.

ix. 1–7. (5) *The cattle of the Egyptians are destroyed.*

9   Then the LORD said unto Moses, Go in unto Pharaoh,
and tell him, Thus saith the LORD, the God of the Hebrews,

---

26. the abomination, i.e. 'to the disgust of.' Animals like
bulls and cows, which the Egyptians held to be sacred (see
Herodotus, II. 38, 41 f., 46), would be sacrificed by the Hebrews.

Let my people go, that they may serve me. For if thou 2
refuse to let them go, and wilt hold them still, behold, the 3
hand of the LORD is upon thy cattle which is in the field,
upon the horses, upon the asses, upon the camels, upon the
herds, and upon the flocks : *there shall be* a very grievous
murrain. And the LORD shall sever between the cattle of 4
Israel and the cattle of Egypt: and there shall nothing
die of all that belongeth to the children of Israel. And 5
the LORD appointed a set time, saying, To-morrow the
LORD shall do this thing in the land. And the LORD did 6
that thing on the morrow, and all the cattle of Egypt died:
but of the cattle of the children of Israel died not one.
And Pharaoh sent, and, behold, there was not so much as 7
one of the cattle of the Israelites dead. But the heart
of Pharaoh was stubborn, and he did not let the people
go.

8-12. (6) *The plague of boils.*

And the LORD said unto Moses and unto Aaron, Take 8
to you handfuls of ashes of the furnace, and let Moses
sprinkle it toward the heaven in the sight of Pharaoh.
And it shall become small dust over all the land of Egypt, 9
and shall be a boil breaking forth with blains upon man
and upon beast, throughout all the land of Egypt. And 10

---

ix. 3. camels were apparently not used by the Egyptians;
those mentioned perhaps belonged to merchantmen (cf. Gen.
xxxvii. 25).

murrain. Cattle plagues sometimes occur in Egypt. This
plague was no doubt the result of the plague of flies.

6. all the cattle. There is some exaggeration here, as some
cattle survived: see *vv.* 19 ff. The two narratives come from
different sources, and the compiler failed to notice the incon-
sistency.

8. ashes, better 'soot,' since it was blown by the wind.

9. boil...blains. Perhaps caused, like the previous plague,
by flies spreading disease. Some writers suggest the *Nile-scab*,
an eruption supposed to be due to infection from the water.

they took ashes of the furnace, and stood before Pharaoh;
and Moses sprinkled it up toward heaven; and it became a
boil breaking forth with blains upon man and upon beast.
11 And the magicians could not stand before Moses because
of the boils; for the boils were upon the magicians, and
12 upon all the Egyptians. And the LORD hardened the heart
of Pharaoh, and he hearkened not unto them; as the LORD
had spoken unto Moses.

13–35. (7) *The hailstorm.*

13   And the LORD said unto Moses, Rise up early in the
morning, and stand before Pharaoh, and say unto him,
Thus saith the LORD, the God of the Hebrews, Let my
14 people go, that they may serve me. For I will this time
send all my plagues upon thine heart, and upon thy servants, and upon thy people; that thou mayest know that
15 there is none like me in all the earth. For now I had put
forth my hand, and smitten thee and thy people with
pestilence, and thou hadst been cut off from the earth:
16 but in very deed for this cause have I made thee to stand,
for to shew thee my power, and that my name may be
17 declared throughout all the earth. As yet exaltest thou
thyself against my people, that thou wilt not let them go?
18 Behold, to-morrow about this time I will cause it to rain
a very grievous hail, such as hath not been in Egypt since
19 the day it was founded even until now. Now therefore send,
hasten in thy cattle and all that thou hast in the field; *for*
every man and beast which shall be found in the field, and
shall not be brought home, the hail shall come down upon
20 them, and they shall die. He that feared the word of the
LORD among the servants of Pharaoh made his servants

---

11. **the magicians**, etc.   The writer seems here almost to see
the humour of the situation.
16. **made thee to stand.**   Cf. St Paul's use in Rom. ix. 17.
18. **since...it was founded.**   Cf. *v.* 24.

and his cattle flee into the houses: and he that regarded 21
not the word of the LORD left his servants and his cattle
in the field.

And the LORD said unto Moses, Stretch forth thine hand 22
toward heaven, that there may be hail in all the land of
Egypt, upon man, and upon beast, and upon every herb
of the field, throughout the land of Egypt. And Moses 23
stretched forth his rod toward heaven : and the LORD sent
thunder and hail, and fire ran down unto the earth ; and
the LORD rained hail upon the land of Egypt. So there 24
was hail, and fire mingled with the hail, very grievous,
such as had not been in all the land of Egypt since it became a nation. And the hail smote throughout all the 25
land of Egypt all that was in the field, both man and beast:
and the hail smote every herb of the field, and brake every
tree of the field. Only in the land of Goshen, where the 26
children of Israel were, was there no hail. And Pharaoh 27
sent, and called for Moses and Aaron, and said unto them,
I have sinned this time: the LORD is righteous, and I
and my people are wicked. Intreat the LORD; for there 28
hath been enough of *these* mighty thunderings and hail;
and I will let you go, and ye shall stay no longer. And 29
Moses said unto him, As soon as I am gone out of the
city, I will spread abroad my hands unto the LORD; the
thunders shall cease, neither shall there be any more hail;
that thou mayest know that the earth is the LORD's. But 30
as for thee and thy servants, I know that ye will not yet
fear the LORD God. And the flax and the barley were 31
smitten : for the barley was in the ear, and the flax was

---

24. mingled with, lit. 'taking hold of itself within': 'flashing
continually amidst' (R.V. m.).

27. righteous...wicked, better 'in the right...the wrong.' The
terms are almost legal.

31. flax was much used in the manufacture of wrappings for
mummies and for linen clothes for priests (cf. Herodotus, II. 37).

32 bolled. But the wheat and the spelt were not smitten : for
33 they were not grown up. And Moses went out of the
city from Pharaoh, and spread abroad his hands unto the
LORD: and the thunders and hail ceased, and the rain
34 was not poured upon the earth. And when Pharaoh saw
that the rain and the hail and the thunders were ceased,
he sinned yet more, and hardened his heart, he and his
35 servants. And the heart of Pharaoh was hardened, and
he did not let the children of Israel go ; as the LORD had
spoken by Moses.

x. 1–20. (8) *The plague of lacusts.*

10 And the LORD said unto Moses, Go in unto Pharaoh :
for I have hardened his heart, and the heart of his servants,
that I might shew these my signs in the midst of them :
2 and that thou mayest tell in the ears of thy son, and of
thy son's son, what things I have wrought upon Egypt,
and my signs which I have done among them ; that ye
3 may know that I am the LORD. And Moses and Aaron
went in unto Pharaoh, and said unto him, Thus saith the
LORD, the God of the Hebrews, How long wilt thou refuse
to humble thyself before me? let my people go, that they
4 may serve me. Else, if thou refuse to let my people go,
5 behold, to-morrow will I bring locusts into thy border : and
they shall cover the face of the earth, that one shall not
be able to see the earth : and they shall eat the residue of
that which is escaped, which remaineth unto you from the
hail, and shall eat every tree which groweth for you out of
6 the field : and thy houses shall be filled, and the houses
of all thy servants, and the houses of all the Egyptians ; as

---

31. bolled. In bud. The plague probably took place towards
the end of January.

32. spelt. A kind of wheat.

x. 4. locusts. A common plague in Palestine but rarer in
Egypt. (For description, etc., see Driver, *Joel*, pp. 37 ff.)

neither thy fathers nor thy fathers' fathers have seen, since
the day that they were upon the earth unto this day. And
he turned, and went out from Pharaoh. And Pharaoh's 7
servants said unto him, How long shall this man be a
snare unto us? let the men go, that they may serve the
LORD their God: knowest thou not yet that Egypt is destroyed? And Moses and Aaron were brought again unto 8
Pharaoh: and he said unto them, Go, serve the LORD your
God: but who are they that shall go? And Moses said, 9
We will go with our young and with our old, with our
sons and with our daughters, with our flocks and with our
herds will we go; for we must hold a feast unto the LORD.
And he said unto them, So be the LORD with you, as I 10
will let you go, and your little ones: look to it; for evil is
before you. Not so: go now ye that are men, and serve 11
the LORD; for that is what ye desire. And they were
driven out from Pharaoh's presence.

And the LORD said unto Moses, Stretch out thine hand 12
over the land of Egypt for the locusts, that they may come
up upon the land of Egypt, and eat every herb of the land,
even all that the hail hath left. And Moses stretched forth 13
his rod over the land of Egypt, and the LORD brought an
east wind upon the land all that day, and all the night;
and when it was morning, the east wind brought the locusts.
And the locusts went up over all the land of Egypt, and 14
rested in all the borders of Egypt; very grievous were
they; before them there were no such locusts as they,
neither after them shall be such. For they covered the face 15

---

7. **snare**, i.e. ' an occasion of destruction.'

11. If **men** only went Pharaoh could be certain that they would
return.   Wives sometimes apparently accompanied the men in
their attendance at festivals (see 1 Sam i. 4 ff. and cf. Deut. xvi.
11), though such attendance was of course not commanded (Exod.
xxiii. 17, etc.).

13. **wind**. Cf. xiv. 21; Numb. xi. 31.

of the whole earth, so that the land was darkened; and
they did eat every herb of the land, and all the fruit of the
trees which the hail had left: and there remained not any
green thing, either tree or herb of the field, through all the
16 land of Egypt. Then Pharaoh called for Moses and Aaron
in haste; and he said, I have sinned against the LORD your
17 God, and against you. Now therefore forgive, I pray thee,
my sin only this once, 'and intreat the LORD your God, that
18 he may take away from me this death only. And he went
19 out from Pharaoh, and intreated the LORD. And the LORD
turned an exceeding strong west wind, which took up the
locusts, and drove them into the Red Sea; there remained
20 not one locust in all the border of Egypt. But the LORD
hardened Pharaoh's heart, and he did not let the children
of Israel go.

21–29. (9) *The great darkness.*

21　　And the LORD said unto Moses, Stretch out thine hand
toward heaven, that there may be darkness over the land
22 of Egypt, even darkness which may be felt. And Moses
stretched forth his hand toward heaven; and there was a
23 thick darkness in all the land of Egypt three days; they
saw not one another, neither rose any from his place for
three days: but all the children of Israel had light in their
24 dwellings. And Pharaoh called unto Moses, and said, Go
ye, serve the LORD; only let your flocks and your herds
25 be stayed: let your little ones also go with you. And Moses
said, Thou must also give into our hand sacrifices and
burnt offerings, that we may sacrifice unto the LORD our
26 God. Our cattle also shall go with us; there shall not an

---

19. strong west wind. Pliny, *Hist. Nat.* XI. 35, is often
quoted as an illustration: 'gregatim sublatae vento in maria aut
stagna decidunt.'

21. darkness. The *Ḥamsīn*, a violent wind which produces
sand-storms, is generally regarded as the natural cause of this
darkness: see the description quoted by McNeile, p. 46.

hoof be left behind; for thereof must we take to serve the
LORD our God; and we know not with what we must serve
the LORD, until we come thither. But the LORD hardened 27
Pharaoh's heart, and he would not let them go. And 28
Pharaoh said unto him, Get thee from me, take heed to thyself, see my face no more; for in the day thou seest my
face thou shalt die. And Moses said, Thou hast spoken 29
well; I will see thy face again no more.

xi. *The last plague threatened.*

And the LORD said unto Moses, Yet one plague more **11**
will I bring upon Pharaoh, and upon Egypt; afterwards
he will let you go hence: when he shall let you go, he shall
surely thrust you out hence altogether. Speak now in the 2
ears of the people, and let them ask every man of his neighbour, and every woman of her neighbour, jewels of silver,
and jewels of gold. And the LORD gave the people favour 3
in the sight of the Egyptians. Moreover the man Moses
was very great in the land of Egypt, in the sight of Pharaoh's
servants, and in the sight of the people.

And Moses said, Thus saith the LORD, About midnight 4
will I go out into the midst of Egypt: and all the firstborn 5
in the land of Egypt shall die, from the firstborn of Pharaoh
that sitteth upon his throne, even unto the firstborn of the
maidservant that is behind the mill; and all the firstborn
of cattle. And there shall be a great cry throughout all the 6
land of Egypt, such as there hath been none like it, nor
shall be like it any more. But against any of the children 7
of Israel shall not a dog move his tongue, against man or
beast: that ye may know how that the LORD doth put a
difference between the Egyptians and Israel. And all these 8

---

xi. 2. every man. An extension of the command in iii. 22.

3. the man Moses. Cf. xxxii. 1; Numb. xii. 3.

7. not a dog, etc. Evidently a proverbial expression. For a
similar usage see Judith xi. 19; cf. also Josh. x. 21 (of men).

thy servants shall come down unto me, and bow down themselves unto me, saying, Get thee out, and all the people that follow thee : and after that I will go out. And he went out from Pharaoh in hot anger.

9 And the LORD said unto Moses, Pharaoh will not hearken unto you : that my wonders may be multiplied in the land 10 of Egypt. And Moses and Aaron did all these wonders before Pharaoh : and the LORD hardened Pharaoh's heart, and he did not let the children of Israel go out of his land.

xii. 1-28. *The celebration of the Passover.*

12 And the LORD spake unto Moses and Aaron in the land 2 of Egypt, saying, This month shall be unto you the beginning of months : it shall be the first month of the year 3 to you. Speak ye unto all the congregation of Israel, saying, In the tenth *day* of this month they shall take to them every man a lamb, according to their fathers' houses, a 4 lamb for an household : and if the household be too little for a lamb, then shall he and his neighbour next unto his house take one according to the number of the souls ; according to every man's eating ye shall make your count 5 for the lamb. Your lamb shall be without blemish, a male of the first year : ye shall take it from the sheep, or from 6 the goats : and ye shall keep it up until the fourteenth day of the same month : and the whole assembly of the congregation of Israel shall kill it at even. And they shall

---

xii. 2. This month, etc. Called by the Canaanite name *Abib* in JE and D, in later writers by the Babylonian, *Nisan* (Neh. ii. 1 ; Esth. iii. 7). P designates the months not by names, but by numbers.

the first month. P uses the Babylonian system of reckoning (cf. Jer. xxxvi. 9 with the present writer's note). The old Hebrew year began in the autumn (cf. xxiii. 16, xxxiv. 22).

3. lamb, or 'kid.' (Heb. *seh*.)

6. at even, lit. 'between the two evenings.' Either between sunset and dark (the natural explanation) ; or from 3 p.m., when the sun's heat begins to decline, and its setting (the traditional explanation).

take of the blood, and put it on the two side posts and on
the lintel, upon the houses wherein they shall eat it. And 8
they shall eat the flesh in that night, roast with fire, and
unleavened bread; with bitter herbs they shall eat it. Eat 9
not of it raw, nor sodden at all with water, but roast with
fire; its head with its legs and with the inwards thereof.
And ye shall let nothing of it remain until the morning; 10
but that which remaineth of it until the morning ye shall
burn with fire. And thus shall ye eat it; with your loins 11
girded, your shoes on your feet, and your staff in your hand:
and ye shall eat it in haste: it is the LORD'S passover.
For I will go through the land of Egypt in that night, and 12
will smite all the firstborn in the land of Egypt, both man
and beast; and against all the gods of Egypt I will execute
judgements: I am the LORD. And the blood shall be to 13
you for a token upon the houses where ye are: and when
I see the blood, I will pass over you, and there shall no
plague be upon you to destroy you, when I smite the land
of Egypt. And this day shall be unto you for a memorial, 14
and ye shall keep it a feast to the LORD: throughout your

---

8. unleavened. For future ages a reminder of their haste and
anxiety: cf. Deut. xvi. 3.

bread, better 'cakes.'

bitter herbs. Elsewhere Numb. ix. 11 and Lam. iii. 15. Later
Israelite thought saw in them a memorial of the bitter bondage
of Egypt.

9. sodden, i.e. 'boiled.'

11. passover (Heb. *pesaḥ*). The origin of the feast and the
meaning of the name are alike uncertain. The feast itself was
perhaps pre-Mosaic, but its celebration at the traditional time of
the Exodus connected it with that event. The Hebrew word
may be derived from *pāsaḥ*, to limp (1 Kings xviii. 21, 26;
cf. Isa. xxxi. 5). See further McNeile, pp. 62 ff.; Driver,
pp. 405 ff.

13. a token. Cf. the sign appointed for Cain, Gen. iv. 15.

I will pass over. Our English word 'Passover' was invented
to reproduce the pun in the original.

14. this day. Not the Passover (the fourteenth day) but the
first day of the Feast of Unleavened Cakes (cf. Lev. xxiii. 5 f.).

generations ye shall keep it a feast by an ordinance for
15 ever. Seven days shall ye eat unleavened bread; even the
first day ye shall put away leaven out of your houses: for
whosoever eateth leavened bread from the first day until
16 the seventh day, that soul shall be cut off from Israel. And
in the first day there shall be to you an holy convocation,
and in the seventh day an holy convocation; no manner
of work shall be done in them, save that which every man
17 must eat, that only may be done of you. And ye shall observe the *feast of* unleavened bread; for in this selfsame
day have I brought your hosts out of the land of Egypt:
therefore shall ye observe this day throughout your gene-
18 rations by an ordinance for ever. In the first *month*, on
the fourteenth day of the month at even, ye shall eat unleavened bread, until the one and twentieth day of the
19 month at even. Seven days shall there be no leaven found
in your houses: for whosoever eateth that which is leavened,
that soul shall be cut off from the congregation of Israel,
whether he be a sojourner, or one that is born in the land.
20 Ye shall eat nothing leavened; in all your habitations shall
ye eat unleavened bread.
21   Then Moses called for all the elders of Israel, and said
unto them, Draw out, and take you lambs according to
22 your families, and kill the passover. And ye shall take a
bunch of hyssop, and dip it in the blood that is in the bason,
and strike the lintel and the two side posts with the blood

---

15. leaven was regarded as a corrupting force: cf. Mark viii.
16; 1 Cor. v. 6, etc.

cut off = excommunicated, put outside the covenant, and therefore perhaps sent into exile. The idea of divine vengeance on
such an offender is also included.

19. sojourner (Heb. *gēr*). 'A man of another tribe or district
who...put himself under the protection of a clan or of a powerful
chief' (Robertson Smith).

22. hyssop = wild marjoram, used as a whisk. See also Lev.
xiv. 4; Numb. xix. 18; and cf. *Aeneid*, VI. 230, where the olive
is used for a like purpose.

that is in the bason; and none of you shall go out of the
door of his house until the morning. For the LORD will 23
pass through to smite the Egyptians; and when he seeth
the blood upon the lintel, and on the two side posts, the
LORD will pass over the door, and will not suffer the destroyer to come in unto your houses to smite you. And ye 24
shall observe this thing for an ordinance to thee and to
thy sons for ever. And it shall come to pass, when ye be 25
come to the land which the LORD will give you, according
as he hath promised, that ye shall keep this service. And 26
it shall come to pass, when your children shall say unto
you, What mean ye by this service? that ye shall say, It 27
is the sacrifice of the LORD'S passover, who passed over
the houses of the children of Israel in Egypt, when he
smote the Egyptians, and delivered our houses. And the
people bowed the head and worshipped. And the children 28
of Israel went and did so; as the LORD had commanded
Moses and Aaron, so did they.

29–36. (10) *The death of the firstborn.*

And it came to pass at midnight, that the LORD smote 29
all the firstborn in the land of Egypt, from the firstborn of
Pharaoh that sat on his throne unto the firstborn of the
captive that was in the dungeon; and all the firstborn of
cattle. And Pharaoh rose up in the night, he, and all his 30
servants, and all the Egyptians; and there was a great cry
in Egypt; for there was not a house where there was not
one dead. And he called for Moses and Aaron by night, 31
and said, Rise up, get you forth from among my people,
both ye and the children of Israel; and go, serve the LORD,
as ye have said. Take both your flocks and your herds, as 32
ye have said, and be gone; and bless me also. And the 33
Egyptians were urgent upon the people, to send them out

---

23. the destroyer. Cf. 2 Sam. xxiv. 16.

of the land in haste; for they said, We be all dead men.
34 And the people took their dough before it was leavened,
their kneadingtroughs being bound up in their clothes upon
35 their shoulders. And the children of Israel did according
to the word of Moses; and they asked of the Egyptians
36 jewels of silver, and jewels of gold, and raiment: and the
LORD gave the people favour in the sight of the Egyptians,
so that they let them have what they asked. And they
spoiled the Egyptians.

37–42. *The flight in haste.*

37   And the children of Israel journeyed from Rameses to
Succoth, about six hundred thousand on foot that were
38 men, beside children. And a mixed multitude went up
also with them; and flocks, and herds, even very much
39 cattle. And they baked unleavened cakes of the dough
which they brought forth out of Egypt, for it was not
leavened; because they were thrust out of Egypt, and
could not tarry, neither had they prepared for themselves
40 any victual. Now the sojourning of the children of Israel,
which they sojourned in Egypt, was four hundred and
41 thirty years. And it came to pass at the end of four hundred and thirty years, even the selfsame day it came to
pass, that all the hosts of the LORD went out from the land

---

34. before it was leavened. Cf. v. 15.

37. Rameses to Succoth. For the former see on i. 11. Succoth
is most probably the *Thukke* of the inscriptions, near to if not
identical with Pithom (i. 11).

six hundred thousand, as in Numb. xi. 21. These figures are
impossible (see McNeile, Driver, etc.), and Petrie suggests that
'thousand' = family.

38. mixed multitude. A source of embarrassment: cf. Numb.
xi. 4.

40. four hundred and thirty years. Cf. Gen. xv. 13 (400
years). P seems to regard Moses and his contemporaries as
being the fourth generation from the patriarchs (see vi. 16 ff.;
Lev. x. 4; Numb. xiv. 1, etc.), and is therefore hardly con-
sistent.

of Egypt. It is a night to be much observed unto the LORD 42
for bringing them out from the land of Egypt: this is that
night of the LORD, to be much observed of all the children
of Israel throughout their generations.

43-51. *The ordinance of the Passover.*

And the LORD said unto Moses and Aaron, This is the 43
ordinance of the passover: there shall no alien eat thereof: but every man's servant that is bought for money, when 44
thou hast circumcised him, then shall he eat thereof. A 45
sojourner and an hired servant shall not eat thereof. In 46
one house shall it be eaten; thou shalt not carry forth
aught of the flesh abroad out of the house; neither shall
ye break a bone thereof. All the congregation of Israel 47
shall keep it. And when a stranger shall sojourn with thee, 48
and will keep the passover to the LORD, let all his males
be circumcised, and then let him come near and keep it;
and he shall be as one that is born in the land: but no
uncircumcised person shall eat thereof. One law shall be 49
to him that is homeborn, and unto the stranger that sojourneth among you. Thus did all the children of Israel; 50
as the LORD commanded Moses and Aaron, so did they.
And it came to pass the selfsame day, that the LORD did 51
bring the children of Israel out of the land of Egypt by
their hosts.

xiii. 1 f. *The firstborn belong to Jehovah.*

And the LORD spake unto Moses, saying, Sanctify unto **13** 2
me all the firstborn, whatsoever openeth the womb among
the children of Israel, both of man and of beast: it is
mine.

---

42. to be much observed, better 'of vigil,' following LXX
προσφυλακή, which is nearer Heb. than Vulg. 'observabilis.'
46. a bone. Cf. Numb. ix. 12; Ps. xxxiv. 20; John xix. 36.
xiii. 2. of man, etc. See on xxii. 29 f.

3–10. *The feast of unleavened bread.*

3 And Moses said unto the people, Remember this day, in which ye came out from Egypt, out of the house of bondage; for by strength of hand the LORD brought you out from this place: there shall no leavened bread be eaten. ⁴₅ This day ye go forth in the month Abib. And it shall be when the LORD shall bring thee into the land of the Canaanite, and the Hittite, and the Amorite, and the Hivite, and the Jebusite, which he sware unto thy fathers to give thee, a land flowing with milk and honey, that thou shalt 6 keep this service in this month. Seven days thou shalt eat unleavened bread, and in the seventh day shall be a feast 7 to the LORD. Unleavened bread shall be eaten throughout the seven days; and there shall no leavened bread be seen with thee, neither shall there be leaven seen with thee, in 8 all thy borders. And thou shalt tell thy son in that day, saying, It is because of that which the LORD did for me 9 when I came forth out of Egypt. And it shall be for a sign unto thee upon thine hand, and for a memorial between thine eyes, that the law of the LORD may be in thy mouth: for with a strong hand hath the LORD brought thee out of 10 Egypt. Thou shalt therefore keep this ordinance in its season from year to year.

11–16. *The dedication of the firstlings.*

11 And it shall be when the LORD shall bring thee into the land of the Canaanite, as he sware unto thee and to thy 12 fathers, and shall give it thee, that thou shalt set apart unto the LORD all that openeth the womb, and every firstling which thou hast that cometh of a beast; the males 13 shall be the LORD's. And every firstling of an ass thou

---

4. Abib = ripening ears, the Canaanitish name; see on xii. 2.

9. sign, possibly by tattooing; cf. Herodotus, II. 113.

memorial. See on *v.* 16.

13. ass. The ass was unclean (i.e. could not be offered to Jehovah), and so a lamb must take its place.

shalt redeem with a lamb ; and if thou wilt not redeem it, then thou shalt break its neck : and all the firstborn of man among thy sons shalt thou redeem. And it shall be when 14 thy son asketh thee in time to come, saying, What is this? that thou shalt say unto him, By strength of hand the LORD brought us out from Egypt, from the house of bondage : and it came to pass, when Pharaoh would hardly let 15 us go, that the LORD slew all the firstborn in the land of Egypt, both the firstborn of man, and the firstborn of beast : therefore I sacrifice to the LORD all that openeth the womb, being males ; but all the firstborn of my sons I redeem. And it shall be for a sign upon thine hand, and for front- 16 lets between thine eyes : for by strength of hand the LORD brought us forth out of Egypt.

XIII. 17—XVIII. The Journeyings up to the Arrival at Sinai.

xiii. 17-22. *The route from Egypt.*

And it came to pass, when Pharaoh had let the people 17 go, that God led them not by the way of the land of the Philistines, although that was near ; for God said, Lest peradventure the people repent when they see war, and they return to Egypt : but God led the people about, by 18

---

13. thy sons. The price in later times was five shekels (Numb. xviii. 15).

14. in time to come, lit. ' to-morrow.'

16. frontlets. The phylacteries or *Tephillīn* of the later Jews (Matt. xxiii. 5) ; charms intended to drive away demons. They contained within them copies of Exod. xiii. 1-16 ; Deut. vi. 4-9, xi. 13-21. To the more spiritual they were a reminder of God ; the Feast of Unleavened Bread (*v.* 9) and the redemption of the firstborn are to be similar reminders.

17. the Philistines. This people did not appear in Canaan until a later period (Sayce, *Early Hist. of Hebrews*, pp. 291 f.) ; the use here is therefore an anachronism.

the way of the wilderness by the Red Sea: and the children of Israel went up armed out of the land of Egypt.

19 And Moses took the bones of Joseph with him: for he had
straitly sworn the children of Israel, saying, God will
surely visit you; and ye shall carry up my bones away

20 hence with you. And they took their journey from Succoth,
and encamped in Etham, in the edge of the wilderness.

21 And the LORD went before them by day in a pillar of cloud,
to lead them the way; and by night in a pillar of fire, to
give them light; that they might go by day and by night:

22 the pillar of cloud by day, and the pillar of fire by night,
departed not from before the people.

xiv. 1–14. *The pursuit of the fugitives.*

14.2   And the LORD spake unto Moses, saying, Speak unto
the children of Israel, that they turn back and encamp before Pi-hahiroth, between Migdol and the sea, before Baal-

3 zephon: over against it shall ye encamp by the sea. And
Pharaoh will say of the children of Israel, They are en-

---

18. Red Sea, lit. 'Sea of Reeds.' The name used in our
English version is derived from the rendering of LXX ἡ ἐρυθρὰ
θάλασσα, the origin of which is obscure.

20. Etham. Probably from the Egyptian *Khetem*, which
means fortress. The actual site is unknown.

21. cloud. In J the cloud is primarily regarded as a guide
(xiv. 19 b; Numb. xiv. 14 b; Deut. i. 33, etc.); in E as a symbol
of the presence of Jehovah (xxxiii. 9 f.; Numb. xi. 25; Deut.
xxxi. 15); in P as a protection (xl. 34 ff.; Numb. ix. 15 ff.).
Mortal leaders have sometimes adopted a similar device; cf. Gib-
bon's account of the expedition of Belisarius against the Vandals:
'the fleet...was guided in their course by his master-galley, con-
spicuous in the day by the redness of its sails, and in the night
by the torches blazing from the masthead.'

xiv. 2. Pi-hahiroth. Pi is the Egyptian for 'house.' The site
of this place and of the two following are all unknown.

Migdol. A Semitic word meaning 'tower'; cf. Etham in
xiii. 20.

Baal-zephon. Also a Semitic word, meaning perhaps 'Lord
of the North.'

tangled in the land, the wilderness hath shut them in. And 4
I will harden Pharaoh's heart, and he shall follow after
them ; and I will get me honour upon Pharaoh, and upon
all his host ; and the Egyptians shall know that I am the
LORD. And they did so. And it was told the king of 5
Egypt that the people were fled : and the heart of Pharaoh
and of his servants was changed towards the people, and
they said, What is this we have done, that we have let
Israel go from serving us? And he made ready his chariot, 6
and took his people with him : and he took six hundred 7
chosen chariots, and all the chariots of Egypt, and captains
over all of them. And the LORD hardened the heart of 8
Pharaoh king of Egypt, and he pursued after the children
of Israel : for the children of Israel went out with an high
hand. And the Egyptians pursued after them, all the 9
horses *and* chariots of Pharaoh, and his horsemen, and his
army, and overtook them encamping by the sea, beside
Pi-hahiroth, before Baal-zephon. And when Pharaoh drew 10
nigh, the children of Israel lifted up their eyes, and, behold,
the Egyptians marched after them : and they were sore
afraid : and the children of Israel cried out unto the LORD.
And they said unto Moses, Because there were no graves 11
in Egypt, hast thou taken us away to die in the wilderness?
wherefore hast thou dealt thus with us, to bring us forth
out of Egypt? Is not this the word that we spake unto thee 12
in Egypt, saying, Let us alone, that we may serve the
Egyptians? For it were better for us to serve the Egyptians,
than that we should die in the wilderness. And Moses said 13

---

5. were fled. Not merely gone on a pilgrimage : cf. vii. 16, etc.
7. captains. Heb. *shālīshīm*, from the root for 'three.' Some
explain the term as meaning the third man in a chariot : the
Egyptians however had only two men in each chariot. Some
kind of military office is evidently intended.
8. high hand. That is 'proudly' or 'defiantly' : cf. Numb.
xv. 30.
12. For similar complaints see Numb. xi. 5, 20, etc.

unto the people, Fear ye not, stand still, and see the salva-
tion of the LORD, which he will work for you to-day: for
the Egyptians whom ye have seen to-day, ye shall see them
14 again no more for ever. The LORD shall fight for you, and
ye shall hold your peace.

15–31. *The crossing of the Red Sea.*

15   And the LORD said unto Moses, Wherefore criest thou
unto me? speak unto the children of Israel, that they go
16 forward. And lift thou up thy rod, and stretch out thine
hand over the sea, and divide it: and the children of
17 Israel shall go into the midst of the sea on dry ground. And
I, behold, I will harden the hearts of the Egyptians, and
they shall go in after them: and I will get me honour upon
Pharaoh, and upon all his host, upon his chariots, and upon
18 his horsemen. And the Egyptians shall know that I am
the LORD, when I have gotten me honour upon Pharaoh,
19 upon his chariots, and upon his horsemen. And the angel
of God, which went before the camp of Israel, removed
and went behind them; and the pillar of cloud removed
20 from before them, and stood behind them: and it came
between the camp of Egypt and the camp of Israel; and
there was the cloud and the darkness, yet gave it light by
night: and the one came not near the other all the night.
21 And Moses stretched out his hand over the sea; and the
LORD caused the sea to go *back* by a strong east wind all

---

15. criest thou. Some words are evidently missing as no cry
of Moses has been recorded.

19. angel of God. See on iii. 2.

20. yet gave it light: lit. 'and it lit up.' The text is apparently defective or disarranged.

21. east wind. The wind drove back the shallow water and
left the dry ground exposed. As in the case of the plagues we
have the providential ordering of natural causes for the well-
being of Israel and for the confounding of their enemies. Josephus tells of a similar story in the life of Alexander the Great
(*Antiq.* II. xvi. 5).

the night, and made the sea dry land, and the waters were
divided. And the children of Israel went into the midst of 22
the sea upon the dry ground: and the waters were a wall
unto them on their right hand, and on their left. And the 23
Egyptians pursued, and went in after them into the midst
of the sea, all Pharaoh's horses, his chariots, and his horsemen. And it came to pass in the morning watch, that the 24
LORD looked forth upon the host of the Egyptians through
the pillar of fire and of cloud, and discomfited the host of
the Egyptians. And he took off their chariot wheels, that 25
they drave them heavily: so that the Egyptians said, Let
us flee from the face of Israel; for the LORD fighteth for
them against the Egyptians.

And the LORD said unto Moses, Stretch out thine hand 26
over the sea, that the waters may come again upon the
Egyptians, upon their chariots, and upon their horsemen.
And Moses stretched forth his hand over the sea, and the 27
sea returned to its strength when the morning appeared;
and the Egyptians fled against it; and the LORD overthrew
the Egyptians in the midst of the sea. And the waters re- 28
turned, and covered the chariots, and the horsemen, even
all the host of Pharaoh that went in after them into the
sea; there remained not so much as one of them. But 29
the children of Israel walked upon dry land in the midst
of the sea; and the waters were a wall unto them on their
right hand, and on their left. Thus the LORD saved Israel 30
that day out of the hand of the Egyptians; and Israel saw

---

24. looked forth. This expression betrays a very primitive
conception of God: cf. the description of Neptune in *Aen.* I.
125 ff.

25. took off. Better with LXX (συνέδησεν), *bound*. The
meaning is evidently that the wheels became fixed in the mud.

27. fled against it. The returning waves came between the
Egyptians and the mainland. The details are obscure because
the scene of the incident is not exactly known. See further,
McNeile, pp. xcv ff.; Driver, pp. 123 ff.

31 the Egyptians dead upon the sea shore. And Israel saw
the great work which the LORD did upon the Egyptians,
and the people feared the|LORD: and they believed in the
LORD, and in his servant Moses.

xv. 1–21. *The triumph song of Moses.*

15   Then sang Moses and the children of Israel this song
unto the LORD, and spake, saying,

> I will sing unto the LORD, for he hath triumphed
> gloriously:
> The horse and his rider hath he thrown into the sea.

2   The LORD is my strength and song,
> And he is become my salvation:
> This is my God, and I will praise him;
> My father's God, and I will exalt him.

3   The LORD is a man of war:
> The LORD is his name.

4   Pharaoh's chariots and his host hath he cast into the
> sea:
> And his chosen captains are sunk in the Red Sea.

5   The deeps cover them:
> They went down into the depths like a stone.

6   Thy right hand, O LORD, is glorious in power,
> Thy right hand, O LORD, dasheth in pieces the enemy.

---

31. they believed. For this function of miracles cf. iv. 1 ff.

xv. 1–18. 'In beauty of style, forceful and nervous language,
and poetical skill, this song is unsurpassed. It stands as one of
the finest specimens of Hebrew lyric poetry' (McNeile). It may
be analysed as follows:
> The subject, 1 b.
> The deliverance by God, 2–5.
> Fuller details of God's action, 6–10.
> The progress of Israel, 11–18.

4. Pharaoh's chariots, etc. There is here no statement that
he himself was drowned (cf. Ps. cxxxvi. 25). The mummy of
Merenptah, the supposed Pharaoh of the Exodus, was discovered
in 1898.

And in the greatness of thine excellency thou over- 7
   throwest them that rise up against thee:
Thou sendest forth thy wrath, it consumeth them as
   stubble.
And with the blast of thy nostrils the waters were 8
   piled up,
The floods stood upright as an heap;
The deeps were congealed in the heart of the sea.
The enemy said,   9
I will pursue, I will overtake, I will divide the spoil:
My lust shall be satisfied upon them;
I will draw my sword, my hand shall destroy them.
Thou didst blow with thy wind, the sea covered them: 10
They sank as lead in the mighty waters.
Who is like unto thee, O LORD, among the gods?   11
Who is like thee, glorious in holiness,
Fearful in praises, doing wonders?
Thou stretchedst out thy right hand,   12
The earth swallowed them.
Thou in thy mercy hast led the people which thou 13
   hast redeemed:
Thou hast guided them in thy strength to thy holy
   habitation.
The peoples have heard, they tremble: 14
Pangs have taken hold on the inhabitants of Philistia.
Then were the dukes of Edom amazed;   15

---

8. the heart of the sea. A common idiom in Hebrew: cf.
Deut. iv. 11; 2 Sam. xviii. 14.
   10. They sank. There is an Arab legend that their spirits
can still be seen moving at the bottom of the sea.
   12. The earth. The context seems to require 'the deep': cf.
Ps. lxix. 15.
   13. This and the following *vv.* evidently come from a time when
Israel was settled in Palestine (so Strack).
   14. tremble, etc. These tenses should all be in the past.
   15. dukes. The heads of clans.

> The mighty men of Moab, trembling taketh hold up-
>   on them:
> All the inhabitants of Canaan are melted away.

16
> Terror and dread falleth upon them;
> By the greatness of thine arm they are as still as a
>   stone;
> Till thy people pass over, O LORD,
> Till the people pass over which thou hast purchased.

17
> Thou shalt bring them in, and plant them in the
>   mountain of thine inheritance,
> The place, O LORD, which thou hast made for thee to
>   dwell in,
> The sanctuary, O LORD, which thy hands have estab-
>   lished.

18
> The LORD shall reign for ever and ever.

19   For the horses of Pharaoh went in with his chariots
and with his horsemen into the sea, and the LORD
brought again the waters of the sea upon them; but the
children of Israel walked on dry land in the midst of the
20 sea. And Miriam the prophetess, the sister of Aaron, took
a timbrel in her hand; and all the women went out after
21 her with timbrels and with dances. And Miriam answered them,

> Sing ye to the LORD, for he hath triumphed gloriously;
> The horse and his rider hath he thrown into the sea.

---

15. mighty men: lit. 'rams.' Cf. Isa. xiv. 9, where 'chief ones'
is lit. 'he-goats.' In an old chronicle of the city of Exeter the
leaders in an uprising are referred to as 'the chief bellwethers.'
    16. still as a stone. Cf. Keats' *Hyperion*, 4 f.
> 'grey-haired Saturn, quiet as a stone,
> Still as the silence round about his lair.'

pass over. Better 'passed through' (see on *v.* 14).
    17. plant them. The same figure is found in Jer. xi. 17;
Ps. xliv. 2, lxxx. 8 ff.
    The sanctuary. The temple of Jerusalem.
    18. shall reign. Cf. Isa xli. 21, xliv. 6.
    20. the prophetess. Cf. Jud. iv. 4 (Deborah).
timbrels...dances. Cf. Jer. xxxi. 4 with the present writer's note.

22–27. *From the Red Sea to Elim.*

And Moses led Israel onward from the Red Sea, and 22
they went out into the wilderness of Shur; and they went
three days in the wilderness, and found no water. And 23
when they came to Marah, they could not drink of the
waters of Marah, for they were bitter: therefore the name
of it was called Marah. And the people murmured against 24
Moses, saying, What shall we drink? And he cried unto 25
the LORD; and the LORD shewed him a tree, and he cast
it into the waters, and the waters were made sweet. There
he made for them a statute and an ordinance, and there
he proved them; and he said, If thou wilt diligently heark- 26
en to the voice of the LORD thy God, and wilt do that
which is right in his eyes, and wilt give ear to his commandments, and keep all his statutes, I will put none of the
diseases upon thee, which I have put upon the Egyptians:
for I am the LORD that healeth thee.

And they came to Elim, where were twelve springs of 27
water, and threescore and ten palm trees: and they encamped there by the waters.

xvi. *The quails and manna.*

And they took their journey from Elim, and all the con- 16
gregation of the children of Israel came unto the wilderness of Sin, which is between Elim and Sinai, on the
fifteenth day of the second month after their departing out

---

22. Shur. (Heb.=wall.) The name of a district on the border
of Egypt, in Numb. xxxiii. 8 called Etham.

23. Marah. Again the site is unknown.

26. the diseases. Cf. Deut. xxviii. 27 (the boil of Egypt). Skin
diseases, ophthalmia, and dysentery are very prevalent in Egypt.

27. Elim=Terebinths, a group of sacred trees perhaps to be
identified with Elath (Deut. ii. 8).

xvi. 1. the wilderness of Sin. Sin seems to be connected in
some way with Sinai, but as no similar name has survived the
position of this desert can only be conjectured: it is perhaps represented by the modern *el-Markhā*.

2 of the land of Egypt. And the whole congregation of the
children of Israel murmured against Moses and against
3 Aaron in the wilderness: and the children of Israel said
unto them, Would that we had died by the hand of the
LORD in the land of Egypt, when we sat by the flesh pots,
when we did eat bread to the full; for ye have brought us
forth into this wilderness, to kill this whole assembly with
4 hunger. Then said the LORD unto Moses, Behold, I will
rain bread from heaven for you; and the people shall go
out and gather a day's portion every day, that I may prove
5 them, whether they will walk in my law, or no. And it
shall come to pass on the sixth day, that they shall pre-
pare that which they bring in, and it shall be twice as
6 much as they gather daily. And Moses and Aaron said
unto all the children of Israel, At even, then ye shall know
that the LORD hath brought you out from the land of Egypt:
7 and in the morning, then ye shall see the glory of the LORD;
for that he heareth your murmurings against the LORD:
8 and what are we, that ye murmur against us? and Moses
said, *This shall be*, when the LORD shall give you in the
evening flesh to eat, and in the morning bread to the full;
for that the LORD heareth your murmurings which ye
murmur against him: and what are we? your murmurings
9 are not against us, but against the LORD. And Moses said
unto Aaron, Say unto all the congregation of the children
of Israel, Come near before the LORD: for he hath heard
10 your murmurings. And it came to pass, as Aaron spake
unto the whole congregation of the children of Israel, that
they looked toward the wilderness, and, behold, the glory

---

4. rain bread. Cf. Ps. lxxviii. 24 f.; John vi. 31.
every day. The same thought is found in the Lord's Prayer.
prove = test.
5. twice as much. In order to avoid labour on the sabbath-
day: cf. *vv.* 23 f.
10. they looked. Cf. Numb. xvi. 42.

of the LORD appeared in the cloud. And the LORD spake 11
unto Moses, saying, I have heard the murmurings of the 12
children of Israel: speak unto them, saying, At even ye
shall eat flesh, and in the morning ye shall be filled with
bread; and ye shall know that I am the LORD your God.
And it came to pass at even, that the quails came up, and 13
covered the camp: and in the morning the dew lay round
about the camp. And when the dew that lay was gone up, 14
behold, upon the face of the wilderness a small round thing,
small as the hoar frost on the ground. And when the 15
children of Israel saw it, they said one to another, What
is it? for they wist not what it was. And Moses said unto
them, It is the bread which the LORD hath given you to
eat. This is the thing which the LORD hath commanded, 16
Gather ye of it every man according to his eating; an
omer a head, according to the number of your persons,
shall ye take it, every man for them which are in his tent.
And the children of Israel did so, and gathered some more, 17
some less. And when they did mete it with an omer, he that 18
gathered much had nothing over, and he that gathered
little had no lack; they gathered every man according
to his eating. And Moses said unto them, Let no man 19
leave of it till the morning. Notwithstanding they heark- 20
ened not unto Moses; but some of them left of it until the

---

12. At even. See on xii. 6.

13. the quails. This notice is evidently detached from its
context as nothing further is said about the quails (see however
Numb. xi.). Quails are a species of partridge and from ancient
times have been known as an article of food: cf. Herodotus, II. 77.

14. round. Better 'flake.' Other descriptions of the manna are
given in *v.* 31 (P) and Numb. xi. 7 ff. (JE). It is suggested that
the sweet juice of the *Tarfa* is meant which exudes from the tree
on summer nights and forms small white grains (see Driver,
pp. 153 ff.).

15. What is it? Another example of a punning explanation
of a word: the real origin of the word *mān* (=manna) is unknown.

18. Cf. St Paul's use of this verse in 2 Cor. viii. 15.

morning, and it bred worms, and stank: and Moses was
21 wroth with them. And they gathered it morning by morning,
every man according to his eating: and when the sun
22 waxed hot, it melted. And it came to pass, that on the
sixth day they gathered twice as much bread, two omers
for each one: and all the rulers of the congregation came
23 and told Moses. And he said unto them, This is that which
the LORD hath spoken, To-morrow is a solemn rest, a holy
sabbath unto the LORD: bake that which ye will bake, and
seethe that which ye will seethe; and all that remaineth
24 over lay up for you to be kept until the morning. And they
laid it up till the morning, as Moses bade: and it did not
25 stink, neither was there any worm therein. And Moses
said, Eat that to-day; for to-day is a sabbath unto the
26 LORD: to-day ye shall not find it in the field. Six days ye
shall gather it; but on the seventh day is the sabbath, in
27 it there shall be none. And it came to pass on the seventh
day, that there went out some of the people for to gather,
28 and they found none. And the LORD said unto Moses,
How long refuse ye to keep my commandments and my
29 laws? See, for that the LORD hath given you the sabbath,
therefore he giveth you on the sixth day the bread of two
days; abide ye every man in his place, let no man go out
30 of his place on the seventh day. So the people rested on
31 the seventh day. And the house of Israel called the name
thereof Manna: and it was like coriander seed, white;
32 and the taste of it was like wafers *made* with honey. And
Moses said, This is the thing which the LORD hath com-

---

21. it melted. Cf. the mystical interpretation of this phe-
nomenon in Wisd. xvi. 27 f. (see Gregg, *ad loc.*).

31. coriander seed. So Numb. xi. 7. A small fruit or seed
about the size of a peppercorn.

taste of...honey. In Numb. xi. 8 fresh oil. A Jewish legend
says that it tasted to each person like his favourite food: cf.
Wisd. xvi. 21.

manded, Let an omerful of it be kept for your generations;
that they may see the bread wherewith I fed you in the
wilderness, when I brought you forth from the land of Egypt.
And Moses said unto Aaron, Take a pot, and put an omer- 33
ful of manna therein, and lay it up before the LORD, to
be kept for your generations. As the LORD commanded 34
Moses, so Aaron laid it up before the Testimony, to be
kept. And the children of Israel did eat the manna forty 35
years, until they came to a land inhabited; they did eat
the manna, until they came unto the borders of the land
of Canaan. Now an omer is the tenth part of an ephah.   36

xvii. 1–7. *The striking of the rock.*

And all the congregation of the children of Israel jour- **17**
neyed from the wilderness of Sin, by their journeys,
according to the commandment of the LORD, and pitched
in Rephidim: and there was no water for the people to
drink. Wherefore the people strove with Moses, and said, 2
Give us water that we may drink. And Moses said unto
them, Why strive ye with me? wherefore do ye tempt the
LORD? And the people thirsted there for water; and the 3
people murmured against Moses, and said, Wherefore hast
thou brought us up out of Egypt, to kill us and our children
and our cattle with thirst? And Moses cried unto the LORD, 4
saying, What shall I do unto this people? they be almost
ready to stone me. And the LORD said unto Moses, Pass 5
on before the people, and take with thee of the elders of

---

34. the Testimony. That is before the ark, so called because
it contained the two tables of the Law. Besides these and the
pot of manna, Aaron's rod (Numb. xvii. 10) was also placed by
the ark. The writer anticipates the making of the ark (xxv. 10).

36. omer. As the ephah = 65 pints, the omer would be about
6½ pints.

xvii. 1. Rephidim. Probably situated in the upper part of the
Wādy Feiran.

Israel; and thy rod, wherewith thou smotest the river, take
6 in thine hand, and go. Behold, I will stand before thee
there upon the rock in Horeb; and thou shalt smite the
rock, and there shall come water out of it, that the people
may drink. And Moses did so in the sight of the elders
7 of Israel. And he called the name of the place Massah,
and Meribah, because of the striving of the children of
Israel, and because they tempted the LORD, saying, Is the
LORD among us, or not?

8-16. *The defeat of Amalek.*

8   Then came Amalek, and fought with Israel in Rephidim.
9 And Moses said unto Joshua, Choose us out men, and go
out, fight with Amalek: to-morrow I will stand on the top
10 of the hill with the rod of God in mine hand. So Joshua
did as Moses had said to him, and fought with Amalek:
and Moses, Aaron, and Hur went up to the top of the hill.
11 And it came to pass, when Moses held up his hand, that
Israel prevailed: and when he let down his hand, Amalek

---

6. Horeb. See on iii. 1. The geographical difficulties are very
great if Horeb = Sinai = *Jebel Mûsā* (see Driver, p. 157).

7. Massah = ' proving' rather than 'tempting,' which in modern
speech suggests 'enticing': cf. *v.* 2. Occurs in Deut. vi. 16,
ix. 22, etc.

Meribah. A similar story is found in Numb. xx. 1-13 (J and P)
with the same name attached to it.

8. Amalek. The Amalekites were a Bedawin tribe and they
quite naturally resented the coming of Israel into a region whose
products were in all probability hardly sufficient for the support
of their own people.

9. Joshua. Here for the first time. Since however he is represented as a grown man and a great warrior the event here described must belong not to the beginning of the wanderings (as
the place of the narrative suggests) but to their close.

the hill. If Rephidim is in the *Wâdy Feiran* this hill is probably *Jebel el-Tahuneh*.

10. Hur. Here and xxiv. 14 (E). Tradition says that he was
the husband of Miriam.

prevailed. But Moses' hands were heavy; and they took 12
a stone, and put it under him, and he sat thereon; and
Aaron and Hur stayed up his hands, the one on the one
side, and the other on the other side; and his hands were
steady until the going down of the sun. And Joshua dis- 13
comfited Amalek and his people with the edge of the sword.
And the LORD said unto Moses, Write this for a memorial 14
in a book, and rehearse it in the ears of Joshua: that I
will utterly blot out the remembrance of Amalek from
under heaven. And Moses built an altar, and called the 15
name of it Jehovah-nissi: and he said, The LORD hath 16
sworn: the LORD will have war with Amalek from generation to generation.

xviii. 1–12. *Jethro visits the Israelites.*

Now Jethro, the priest of Midian, Moses' father in law, 18
heard of all that God had done for Moses, and for Israel
his people, how that the LORD had brought Israel out of
Egypt. And Jethro, Moses' father in law, took Zipporah,
Moses' wife, after he had sent her away, and her two sons; 2
of which the name of one was Gershom; for he said, I 3
have been a sojourner in a strange land: and the name 4
of the other was Eliezer; for *he said*, The God of my father
was my help, and delivered me from the sword of Pharaoh:
and Jethro, Moses' father in law, came with his sons and 5

---

12. were steady: lit. 'steadiness.' In other passages the word
has an ethical sense 'faithfulness.'

13. with the edge of the sword (lit. 'according to the mouth
of the sword') = 'without quarter.'

14. Write this. The art of writing is very ancient but we do
not know how widespread it was in Israel (see the author's note
on Jer. xxxvi. 1–8).

15. Jehovah-nissi: lit. 'J. is my banner.' Cf. Gen. xxii. 14;
Jud. vi. 24.

16. See 1 Sam. xv. 2 f.

xviii. 1. Jethro. See on ii. 18.

his wife unto Moses into the wilderness where he was en-
6 camped, at the mount of God: and he said unto Moses,
I thy father in law Jethro am come unto thee, and thy wife,
7 and her two sons with her. And Moses went out to meet
his father in law, and did obeisance, and kissed him ; and
they asked each other of their welfare; and they came
8 into the tent. And Moses told his father in law all that
the LORD had done unto Pharaoh and to the Egyptians
for Israel's sake, all the travail that had come upon them
9 by the way, and how the LORD delivered them. And Jethro
rejoiced for all the goodness which the LORD had done to
Israel, in that he had delivered them out of the hand of the
10 Egyptians. And Jethro said, Blessed be the LORD, who
hath delivered you out of the hand of the Egyptians, and
out of the hand of Pharaoh ; who hath delivered the people
11 from under the hand of the Egyptians. Now I know that
the LORD is greater than all gods : yea, in the thing
12 wherein they dealt proudly against them. And Jethro,
Moses' father in law, took a burnt offering and sacrifices
for God : and Aaron came, and all the elders of Israel, to
eat bread with Moses' father in law before God.

13–27. *The appointment of judges.*

13 And it came to pass on the morrow, that Moses sat to
judge the people : and the people stood about Moses from
14 the morning unto the evening. And when Moses' father
in law saw all that he did to the people, he said, What is
this thing that thou doest to the people? why sittest thou

---

5. the mount of God = Horeb. As the Israelites only reach Sinai
in xix. 1 f., this narrative, like that which precedes it, is evidently
displaced.

11. than all gods. Some scholars think that Moses derived
his knowledge of Jehovah from Jethro. In this incident the latter
certainly seems to take the lead.

12. to eat bread, etc. That is to share with them in a sacrificial meal.

thyself alone, and all the people stand about thee from
morning unto even? And Moses said unto his father in 15
law, Because the people come unto me to inquire of God:
when they have a matter, they come unto me; and I judge 16
between a man and his neighbour, and I make them know
the statutes of God, and his laws. And Moses' father in 17
law said unto him, The thing that thou doest is not good.
Thou wilt surely wear away, both thou, and this people 18
that is with thee: for the thing is too heavy for thee; thou
art not able to perform it thyself alone. Hearken now 19
unto my voice, I will give thee counsel, and God be with
thee: be thou for the people to God-ward, and bring thou
the causes unto God: and thou shalt teach them the 20
statutes and the laws, and shalt shew them the way wherein
they must walk, and the work that they must do. Moreover 21
thou shalt provide out of all the people able men, such as
fear God, men of truth, hating unjust gain; and place
such over them, to be rulers of thousands, rulers of hundreds, rulers of fifties, and rulers of tens: and let them 22
judge the people at all seasons: and it shall be, that every
great matter they shall bring unto thee, but every small
matter they shall judge themselves: so shall it be easier
for thyself, and they shall bear *the burden* with thee. If 23
thou shalt do this thing, and God command thee so, then
thou shalt be able to endure, and all this people also shall

---

15. inquire of God. The answers would often be given by lot
in early times; later the priest would answer according to his
own judgment and the traditional law.

16. statutes...laws. Definite rules, and occasional directions.

21. McNeile points out that in order to provide for the whole
congregation of 600,000 men nearly 80,000 rulers would be required. The scheme is an ideal and not a practical one

22. every small matter. Edgar the great Saxon law-giver
found it necessary 'to forbid recourse to the king's audience until
the local means of obtaining justice had been exhausted'; Stubbs,
Constitutional Hist. I. p. 229.

24 go to their place in peace. So Moses hearkened to the
voice of his father in law, and did all that he had said.

25 And Moses chose able men out of all Israel, and made
them heads over the people, rulers of thousands, rulers of

26 hundreds, rulers of fifties, and rulers of tens. And they
judged the people at all seasons: the hard causes they
brought unto Moses, but every small matter they judged

27 themselves. And Moses let his father in law depart; and
he went his way into his own land.

XIX–XL. ISRAEL AT SINAI.

xix. *The arrival and the theophany.*

19 In the third month after the children of Israel were
gone forth out of the land of Egypt, the same day came

2 they into the wilderness of Sinai. And when they were
departed from Rephidim, and were come to the wilderness
of Sinai, they pitched in the wilderness; and there Israel

3 camped before the mount. And Moses went up unto God,
and the LORD called unto him out of the mountain, saying,
Thus shalt thou say to the house of Jacob, and tell the

4 children of Israel; Ye have seen what I did unto the Egyptians, and how I bare you on eagles' wings, and brought

---

xix. 1. the wilderness of Sinai. The tradition which places
the mount of the lawgiving in the Sinai peninsula only goes back
to the third century A.D. Sayce suggests a site on the east side
of the Gulf of Akaba, and other scholars would bring it near to
Kadesh (e.g. McNeile). The insufficiency of the geographical
data at our disposal and the apparent difference of tradition in the
various sources make a decision almost impossible: see McNeile,
pp. ci ff.; Driver, pp. 177 ff.; Sayce, *Early History of the Hebrews*,
pp. 186 ff.

2. the mount. The traditional site in the Sinai peninsula is
Jebel Mūsā but many writers favour *Jebel Serbāl*: see Driver,
pp. 186 ff.

3. Jacob as synonym for Israel is poetic.

4. eagles' wings. Really the griffon-vulture.

you unto myself. Now therefore, if ye will obey my voice 5
indeed, and keep my covenant, then ye shall be a peculiar
treasure unto me from among all peoples : for all the earth
is mine : and ye shall be unto me a kingdom of priests, 6
and an holy nation. These are the words which thou shalt
speak unto the children of Israel. And Moses came and 7
called for the elders of the people, and set before them all
these words which the LORD commanded him. And all 8
the people answered together, and said, All that the LORD
hath spoken we will do. And Moses reported the words
of the people unto the LORD. And the LORD said unto 9
Moses, Lo, I come unto thee in a thick cloud, that the
people may hear when I speak with thee, and may also
believe thee for ever. And Moses told the words of the
people unto the LORD. And the LORD said unto Moses, 10
Go unto the people, and sanctify them to-day and to-morrow,
and let them wash their garments, and be ready against 11
the third day : for the third day the LORD will come down
in the sight of all the people upon mount Sinai. And thou 12
shalt set bounds unto the people round about, saying, Take
heed to yourselves, that ye go not up into the mount, or
touch the border of it : whosoever toucheth the mount shall
be surely put to death : no hand shall touch him, but he 13
shall surely be stoned, or shot through ; whether it be beast

---

5. my covenant. J and E speak of a covenant made at Sinai,
P refers back to that made with the patriarchs. See list of cove-
nants in Driver, pp. 175 f.

a peculiar treasure : lit. 'a special possession.' LXX renders
λαὸς περιούσιος : cf. Tit. ii. 14 ; Eph. i. 14.

6. of priests. Universal access to God : cf. 1 Pet. ii. 5, 9 ;
Rev. i. 6, v. 10, xx. 6.

10. sanctify them. Cf. Numb. xi. 18. According to later
Jewish writers baptism was included in the process ; see Eder-
sheim, *Life and Times of Jesus*, etc. I. p. 274.

13. no hand, etc. Baentsch suggests that the offender by
touching that which was holy would become *taboo* or holy himself
(cf. xxix. 37 b), and therefore 'infectious.'

or man, it shall not live : when the trumpet soundeth long,
14 they shall come up to the mount. And Moses went down
from the mount unto the people, and sanctified the people ;
15 and they washed their garments. And he said unto the
people, Be ready against the third day : come not near a
16 woman. And it came to pass on the third day, when it
was morning, that there were thunders and lightnings,
and a thick cloud upon the mount, and the voice of a
trumpet exceeding loud ; and all the people that were in
17 the camp trembled. And Moses brought forth the people
out of the camp to meet God ; and they stood at the nether
18 part of the mount. And mount Sinai was altogether on
smoke, because the LORD descended upon it in fire : and
the smoke thereof ascended as the smoke of a furnace,
19 and the whole mount quaked greatly. And when the voice
of the trumpet waxed louder and louder, Moses spake, and
20 God answered him by a voice. And the LORD came down
upon mount Sinai, to the top of the mount : and the LORD
called Moses to the top of the mount ; and Moses went
21 up. And the LORD said unto Moses, Go down, charge the
people, lest they break through unto the LORD to gaze,
22 and many of them perish. And let the priests also, which
come near to the LORD, sanctify themselves, lest the LORD
23 break forth upon them. And Moses said unto the LORD,
The people cannot come up to mount Sinai : for thou didst
charge us, saying, Set bounds about the mount, and sanc-
24 tify it. And the LORD said unto him, Go, get thee down ;
and thou shalt come up, thou, and Aaron with thee : but
let not the priests and the people break through to come

---

13. trumpet, 'ram's horn'; in *v.* 16 a different word is used.
16. thunders, etc. Cf. Ps. xviii. 7 ff., l. 3, xcvii. 3 ff.; Mic.
i. 3 f.: Hab. iii. 3 ff.
the voice of a trumpet. This was no earthly instrument : cf.
1 Thess. iv. 16; 1 Cor. xv. 52 ; Rev. viii. 2 ff.
22. priests. J recognises them already : cf. xxxii. 29.

up unto the LORD, lest he break forth upon them. So 25
Moses went down unto the people, and told them.

XX. 1–21. *The Decalogue.*

And God spake all these words saying,   **20**

I am the LORD thy God, which brought thee out of the 2
land of Egypt, out of the house of bondage.

Thou shalt have none other gods before me.   3

Thou shalt not make unto thee a graven image, nor *the* 4
likeness of any form that is in heaven above, or that is in
the earth beneath, or that is in the water under the earth:
thou shalt not bow down thyself unto them, nor serve them: 5
for I the LORD thy God am a jealous God, visiting the
iniquity of the fathers upon the children, upon the third
and upon the fourth generation of them that hate me; and 6
shewing mercy unto thousands, of them that love me and
keep my commandments.

XX. 1. these words. Cf. also Deut. v. 6–21 and note the verbal
differences.

3. before me: lit. 'in my presence.' God must not be dis-
honoured by seeing other gods.

4. graven image. An idol carved in wood or stone.
under the earth. The O.T. writers thought of the earth as
flat and as resting upon the water (cf. Gen. vii. 11, xlix. 25;
Ps. cxxxvi. 6). Xenophon tells us that the Syrians regarded the
fish in the river Chalus as gods (*Anab.* I. iv. 9); other instances
of the worship of marine animals are not uncommon (see W. R.
Smith's *Rel. of the Semites*[2], pp. 173 ff., 292 f.).

5. jealous God. One who will not suffer His worship to be
given to another.
upon the children. 'The study of natural science is daily
making it clearer that God works by and in natural laws, so that
causes produce results, and the suffering of children by reason
of their father's sins is a daily spectacle. It must be remembered,
however, that to the Hebrew writer the words had reference only
to the external consequences of sin, and not to any feeling of
anger on God's part against innocent sufferers.' (McNeile.) Cf.
the present writer's *Jeremiah*, pp. liv f. and 238.

6. thousands: lit. 'a thousand generations.' The effect of a
life of goodness extends further than that of a life of sin.

7   Thou shalt not take the name of the LORD thy God in
     vain; for the LORD will not hold him guiltless that taketh
     his name in vain.

8
9   Remember the sabbath day, to keep it holy. Six days
10   shalt thou labour, and do all thy work: but the seventh
     day is a sabbath unto the LORD thy God: *in it* thou shalt
     not do any work, thou, nor thy son, nor thy daughter, thy
     manservant, nor thy maidservant, nor thy cattle, nor thy
11   stranger that is within thy gates: for in six days the LORD
     made heaven and earth, the sea, and all that in them is,
     and rested the seventh day: wherefore the LORD blessed
     the sabbath day, and hallowed it.

12   Honour thy father and thy mother: that thy days may
     be long upon the land which the LORD thy God giveth
     thee.

13   Thou shalt do no murder.

---

7. in vain. The holy name of God is to be reverenced and not
to be used in a sinful or unworthy manner.

10. a sabbath. Heb. *shabbāth*, is apparently derived from a
root meaning to desist or cease (cf. the use in Isa. xiv. 4, xxiv. 8).
It is, however, difficult to separate the institution from the Babylonian *shabbatum*, a day upon which the gods ceased from anger
(see McNeile, pp. 121 f.). The seventh day was a day of rest
from work with the Babylonians, especially in early times.

11. This reason is based on Gen. ii. 3 (P). In Deut. v. 14 a
characteristically humanitarian motive is substituted.

12-17. The order of the last six commandments is not quite fixed,
as the following table of different arrangements clearly shews:

Luke xviii. 20.	7th,	6th,	8th,	9th,	5th.
Rom. xiii. 9.	7th,	6th,	8th,	10th.	
Jas. ii. 11.	7th,	6th.			

Philo and some Heb. MSS. follow this latter order and different MSS. of LXX make still further changes: see the fuller table
in McNeile, p. 119.

12. Cf. Plato, *Legg.* IV. 717 C–D; Aristotle, *Eth. Nic.* IX. 2, 8.

thy days may be long. A similar promise is made to anyone
who shall leave the mother bird in her nest (Deut. xxii. 7). The
Rabbis said that God had only revealed the reward for keeping
the greatest and the least of the commandments.

13. Cf. Matt. v. 21 ff.

Thou shalt not commit adultery. 14

Thou shalt not steal. 15

Thou shalt not bear false witness against thy neighbour. 16

Thou shalt not covet thy neighbour's house, thou shalt 17
not covet thy neighbour's wife, nor his manservant, nor his
maidservant, nor his ox, nor his ass, nor any thing that is
thy neighbour's.

And all the people saw the thunderings, and the light- 18
nings, and the voice of the trumpet, and the mountain
smoking: and when the people saw it, they trembled, and
stood afar off. And they said unto Moses, Speak thou with 19
us, and we will hear: but let not God speak with us, lest
we die. And Moses said unto the people, Fear not: for 20
God is come to prove you, and that his fear may be before
you, that ye sin not. And the people stood afar off, and 21
Moses drew near unto the thick darkness where God was.

xx. 22–xxiii. 19. *Miscellaneous regulations.*

And the LORD said unto Moses, Thus thou shalt say 22
unto the children of Israel, Ye yourselves have seen that
I have talked with you from heaven. Ye shall not make 23
other gods with me; gods of silver, or gods of gold, ye
shall not make unto you. An altar of earth thou shalt make 24
unto me, and shalt sacrifice thereon thy burnt offerings,

---

16. false witness. One of the commonest crimes in the East
in all ages.

17. wife. According to this version the wife is part of the
husband's household or property: Deut. v. 21 more humanely
mentions the wife first.

19. Speak thou. Cf. Deut. v. 22 ff.

22. from heaven. God dwells in the high and holy place
(Isa. lvii. 15) and those who worship Him must shun the use
of idols.

24. altar of earth. Such altars were apparently common
amongst the Romans: cf. *Aen.* XII. 118 f. *arae gramineae*;
Horace, *Odes*, III. viii. 3 f.

burnt offerings. Heb. *'olōth*, from a root = to ascend; the
whole beast was consumed by fire.

and thy peace offerings, thy sheep, and thine oxen: in
every place where I record my name I will come unto thee
25 and I will bless thee. And if thou make me an altar of
stone, thou shalt not build it of hewn stones: for if thou
26 lift up thy tool upon it, thou hast polluted it. Neither
shalt thou go up by steps unto mine altar, that thy nakedness be not discovered thereon.

21   Now these are the judgements which thou shalt set before them.

2   If thou buy an Hebrew servant, six years he shall serve:
3 and in the seventh he shall go out free for nothing. If he

---

24. peace offerings. Heb. *shelāmīm*. The English rendering con-
nects the word with *shālōm* = peace, but the derivation is uncertain.
The peace offering differed from the burnt offering in being a
sacred meal, the worshipper (later the priest also) consuming a
portion.

record my name (= 'cause my name to be remembered'). Where-
ever God's presence has been manifested an altar may be erected:
cf. xvii. 15; Gen. xxviii. 18. The ancient Semites were very con-
servative in such matters and new temples could only be erected
'where the godhead had given unmistakable evidence of his
presence' (W. R. Smith, *R. l. of the Semites²*, p. 115).

25. altar of stone. Cf. 1 Sam. xiv. 32 ff. Many ancient rock-
altars have been found in Palestine.

hewn stones. So Deut. xxvii. 5 f. and cf. 1 Kings vi. 7.

26. Cf. the later provision, xxviii. 42.

xxi. 1. judgements. By this term is meant 'legal decisions'
which would when given have the force of precedents: cf. in
English jurisprudence the distinction between statutory and case
law.

2. servant, i.e. 'slave.' Hebrews might be slaves by being
born such (*v.* 4), or through being sold by their parents, or by
their own act (Lev. xxv. 39). Theft might be punished by en-
slavement (xxii. 3). Notice that the laws here, like those in
Deut. xv. 12 ff., refer only to natives; foreign slaves are dealt with
very briefly in Lev. xxv. 44 ff. Later legislation tries to forbid
the possession of Hebrew slaves altogether (Lev. xxv. 39 ff.). In
giving rights to slaves the Hebrews were in advance of most
ancient peoples.

seventh Cf. Deut. xv. 12; Jer. xxxiv. 14.

free. Deut. xv. 13 f. goes further and makes the master give a
liberal present.

come in by himself, he shall go out by himself: if he be
married, then his wife shall go out with him. If his master 4
give him a wife, and she bear him sons or daughters; the
wife and her children shall be her master's, and he shall
go out by himself. But if the servant shall plainly say, I 5
love my master, my wife, and my children; I will not go
out free: then his master shall bring him unto God, and 6
shall bring him to the door, or unto the door post; and
his master shall bore his ear through with an awl; and he
shall serve him for ever.

And if a man sell his daughter to be a maidservant, she 7
shall not go out as the menservants do. If she please not 8
her master, who hath espoused her to himself, then shall
he let her be redeemed: to sell her unto a strange people
he shall have no power, seeing he hath dealt deceitfully
with her. And if he espouse her unto his son, he shall deal 9
with her after the manner of daughters. If he take him 10
another *wife*; her food, her raiment, and her duty of
marriage, shall he not diminish. And if he do not these 11
three unto her, then shall she go out for nothing, without
money.

He that smiteth a man, so that he die, shall surely be 12
put to death. And if a man lie not in wait, but God 13

---

3. married: lit. 'lord of a wife.' An idiomatic use characteristic of E.

6. unto God, margin 'the judges'; cf. xxii. 8 f.; 1 Sam. ii. 25.
The expression may perhaps mean 'to a sanctuary,' though
Baentsch refers it to the household gods (*terāphīm* or Penates).
In Deut. xv. 16 f., since a journey to Jerusalem in such cases
would often be out of the question, the phrase is omitted.

the door. Probably the door of the master's house though it is
hard to reconcile this with a visit to a sanctuary.

bore his ear. In Deut. xv. 17 the ear is attached to the door.
J. G. Frazer has a chapter on this ceremony in *Folk-Lore in O.T.*
III. pp. 165 ff.

7. maidservant. That is a female slave, and in practice, a
concubine.

8. strange, i.e. 'foreign.'

deliver *him* into his hand; then I will appoint thee a place
14 whither he shall flee. And if a man come presumptuously
upon his neighbour, to slay him with guile; thou shalt
take him from mine altar, that he may die.

15 And he that smiteth his father, or his mother, shall be
surely put to death.

16 And he that stealeth a man, and selleth him, or if he be
found in his hand, he shall surely be put to death.

17 And he that curseth his father, or his mother, shall surely
be put to death.

18 And if men contend, and one smiteth the other with a
stone, or with his fist, and he die not, but keep his bed:
19 if he rise again, and walk abroad upon his staff, then shall
he that smote him be quit: only he shall pay for the loss
of his time, and shall cause him to be thoroughly healed.

20 And if a man smite his servant, or his maid, with a rod,
and he die under his hand; he shall surely be punished.
21 Notwithstanding, if he continue a day or two, he shall
not be punished: for he is his money.

22 And if men strive together, and hurt a woman with child,
so that her fruit depart, and yet no mischief follow; he

---

13. a place. An asylum; in earlier times at a sanctuary (cf.
v. 14), later in 'cities of refuge' (Deut. xix. 1 ff.; Numb. xxxv.
6, 11 ff.). A similar custom prevailed amongst the Greeks and
Romans (Tacitus, *Ann.* III. 60).

15. smiteth. The murder of a parent would come under the
previous law unless, like Solon, the Hebrews regarded the murder
of a parent as an impossible crime and so did not legislate for it
(cf. Cicero, *Pro Rosc.* § 70).

16. put to death. So amongst the Greeks (Xenophon, *Memor*,
1. ii. 62).

17. curseth. Cf. Matt. xv. 4.

18. fist. This rendering follows LXX, Vulg. etc. Some
scholars suggest 'shovel' or 'hoe,' which is also possible.

20. be punished. The Romans under the Republic had the
right of killing their slaves (Plutarch, *Cato*, XXI.; though here
the opinion of the other slaves is asked, a somewhat unusual
proceeding one imagines).

shall be surely fined, according as the woman's husband shall lay upon him; and he shall pay as the judges determine. But if any mischief follow, then thou shalt give life 23 for life, eye for eye, tooth for tooth, hand for hand, foot for 24 foot, burning for burning, wound for wound, stripe for 25 stripe.

And if a man smite the eye of his servant, or the eye of 26 his maid, and destroy it; he shall let him go free for his eye's sake. And if he smite out his manservant's tooth, 27 or his maidservant's tooth; he shall let him go free for his tooth's sake.

And if an ox gore a man or a woman, that they die, the 28 ox shall be surely stoned, and his flesh shall not be eaten; but the owner of the ox shall be quit. But if the ox were 29 wont to gore in time past, and it hath been testified to his owner, and he hath not kept him in, but that he hath killed a man or a woman; the ox shall be stoned, and his owner also shall be put to death. If there be laid on him a ransom, 30 then he shall give for the redemption of his life whatsoever is laid upon him. Whether he have gored a son, or have 31 gored a daughter, according to this judgement shall it be done unto him. If the ox gore a manservant or a maid- 32 servant; he shall give unto their master thirty shekels of silver, and the ox shall be stoned.

And if a man shall open a pit, or if a man shall dig a 33 pit and not cover it, and an ox or an ass fall therein, the 34

---

24. eye for eye, etc. Cf. Matt. v. 38. The *lex talionis* is a stage towards better things, since it limits the punishment or vengeance.

28. an ox, etc. ' In mediaeval Europe animals charged with causing a death were often tried in a court of law, and, if found guilty, killed; a cow was executed in this way in France as late as 1740' (Driver).

32. thirty shekels. Cf. Zech. xi. 13; Matt. xxvii. 9 f. He who took upon Him the form of a slave (Phil. ii. 7) was sold at the price of a slave.

owner of the pit shall make it good ; he shall give money unto the owner of them, and the dead *beast* shall be his.

35 And if one man's ox hurt another's, that he die ; then they shall sell the live ox, and divide the price of it; and 36 the dead also they shall divide. Or if it be known that the ox was wont to gore in time past, and his owner hath not kept him in ; he shall surely pay ox for ox, and the dead *beast* shall be his own.

22 If a man shall steal an ox, or a sheep, and kill it, or sell it ; he shall pay five oxen for an ox, and four sheep for a 2 sheep. If the thief be found breaking in, and be smitten 3 that he die, there shall be no bloodguiltiness for him. If the sun be risen upon him, there shall be bloodguiltiness for him: he should make restitution; if he have nothing, 4 then he shall be sold for his theft. If the theft be found in his hand alive, whether it be ox, or ass, or sheep; he shall pay double.

5 If a man shall cause a field or vineyard to be eaten, and shall let his beast loose, and it feed in another man's field; of the best of his own field, and of the best of his own vineyard, shall he make restitution.

6 If fire break out, and catch in thorns, so that the shocks of corn, or the standing corn, or the field, be consumed ; he that kindled the fire shall surely make restitution.

7 If a man shall deliver unto his neighbour money or stuff to keep, and it be stolen out of the man's house; if the 8 thief be found, he shall pay double. If the thief be not found, then the master of the house shall come near unto God, *to see* whether he have not put his hand unto his

---

xxii. 1. five...four. The principle of multiple restitution is found in the Code of Ḥammurabi.

2. breaking in. Lit. ' digging through.'

7. to keep. The disposal of savings or property was a real problem before the days of banks and depositories.

8. unto God. Some kind of ordeal seems to be suggested : cf. Numb. v. 11 ff.

neighbour's goods. For every matter of trespass, whether 9
it be for ox, for ass, for sheep, for raiment, *or* for any
manner of lost thing, whereof one saith, This is it, the
cause of both parties shall come before God; he whom
God shall condemn shall pay double unto his neighbour.

If a man deliver unto his neighbour an ass, or an ox, or 10
a sheep, or any beast, to keep; and it die, or be hurt, or
driven away, no man seeing it: the oath of the LORD shall 11
be between them both, whether he hath not put his hand
unto his neighbour's goods; and the owner thereof shall
accept it, and he shall not make restitution. But if it be 12
stolen from him, he shall make restitution unto the owner
thereof. If it be torn in pieces, let him bring it for witness; 13
he shall not make good that which was torn.

And if a man borrow aught of his neighbour, and it be 14
hurt, or die, the owner thereof not being with it, he shall
surely make restitution. If the owner thereof be with it, he 15
shall not make it good: if it be an hired thing, it came for
its hire.

And if a man entice a virgin that is not betrothed, and 16
lie with her, he shall surely pay a dowry for her to be his
wife. If her father utterly refuse to give her unto him, he 17
shall pay money according to the dowry of virgins.

Thou shalt not suffer a sorceress to live.   18

Whosoever lieth with a beast shall surely be put to 19
death.

He that sacrificeth unto any god, save unto the LORD 20
only, shall be utterly destroyed. And a stranger shalt thou 21

---

17. dowry. The father had to be compensated for the damage
to his property, for as such an unmarried daughter was regarded.

18. sorceress. Witches were burnt in England up to 1716.

20. utterly destroyed: lit. 'devoted.' With the Hebrews to
devote an object to Jehovah usually involved its destruction :
cf. Deut. ii. 34 f., xiii. 12 ff.; Jos. vi. 17 ff.; 1 Sam. xv. 3, 9.

not wrong, neither shalt thou oppress him: for ye were
22 strangers in the land of Egypt. Ye shall not afflict any
23 widow, or fatherless child. If thou afflict them in any wise,
and they cry at all unto me, I will surely hear their cry;
24 and my wrath shall wax hot, and I will kill you with the
sword; and your wives shall be widows, and your children
fatherless.

25   If thou lend money to any of my people with thee that
is poor, thou shalt not be to him as a creditor; neither shall
26 ye lay upon him usury. If thou at all take thy neighbour's
garment to pledge, thou shalt restore it unto him by that
27 the sun goeth down: for that is his only covering, it is his
garment for his skin: wherein shall he sleep? and it shall
come to pass, when he crieth unto me, that I will hear;
for I am gracious.

28   Thou shalt not revile God, nor curse a ruler of thy people.
29 Thou shalt not delay to offer of the abundance of thy fruits,
and of thy liquors. The firstborn of thy sons shalt thou

---

25. usury, better 'interest.' The prohibition of interest in the
case of a charitable loan should not be extended so as to include
the modern system of interest on investments.

26. Cf. Deut. xxiv. 12 f.; Amos ii. 8.

28. revile God. Better 'judges' in view of the parallelism.
Josephus took it to refer to heathen gods, which were not to be
blasphemed nor their temples robbed (*Antiq.* IV. viii. 10), an
offence to which the later Jews were supposed to be prone
(Ramsay, *Church in Rom. Emp.* p. 144).

a ruler. Cf. Acts xxiii. 5.

29. fruits...liquors: lit. 'fulness...juice.' LXX 'the first
fruits of thy threshing-floor and of thy wine-press.'

of thy sons. The custom of sacrificing the first-born seems to
be very ancient and widespread. The offering was probably
made for the same reason as in the case of firstlings as a thank-
offering to God and in expectation of a large number of children
in return (cf. W. R. Smith, *Rel. of Semites*[2], pp. 464 f.). Amongst
the Hebrews in historic times the actual sacrifice of children was
regarded as very exceptional (cf. Jud. xi.), though it seems to
have been more common in the last days of the kingdom of Judah
(Jer. vii. 31, xix. 5, xxxii. 35; Ezek. xvi. 20 f.), doubtless through
the influence of foreign cults.

give unto me. Likewise shalt thou do with thine oxen, *and* 30
with thy sheep : seven days it shall be with its dam ; on
the eighth day thou shalt give it me. And ye shall be holy 31
men unto me : therefore ye shall not eat any flesh that is
torn of beasts in the field ; ye shall cast it to the dogs.

Thou shalt not take up a false report : put not thine hand **23**
with the wicked to be an unrighteous witness. Thou shalt 2
not follow a multitude to do evil ; neither shalt thou speak
in a cause to turn aside after a multitude to wrest *judge-*
ment : neither shalt thou favour a poor man in his cause. 3

If thou meet thine enemy's ox or his ass going astray, 4
thou shalt surely bring it back to him again. If thou see 5
the ass of him that hateth thee lying under his burden, and
wouldest forbear to help him, thou shalt surely help with
him.

Thou shalt not wrest the judgement of thy poor in his 6
cause. Keep thee far from a false matter ; and the innocent 7
and righteous slay thou not : for I will not justify the
wicked. And thou shalt take no gift : for a gift blindeth 8
them that have sight, and perverteth the words of the
righteous. And a stranger shalt thou not oppress : for ye 9
know the heart of a stranger, seeing ye were strangers in
the land of Egypt.

---

30. oxen, etc. There is no mention here of the firstlings of
unclean animals : cf. xiii. 13.

eighth day. Cf. Lev. xxii. 27.

31. holy. Originally this word had no reference to *moral*
perfection ; it referred rather to *ceremonial* requirements. As the
conception of God became higher the avoidance of evil as well as
of ritual defilement was emphasised.

torn. Such flesh would be unclean by the regulations of
Deut. xii. 16, etc. According to Deut. xiv. 21 it could be eaten
by non-Israelites.

xxiii. 3. poor. A slight change in Heb. gives the much more
probable reading of 'great.'

4. enemy's. The Rabbis limited this to a Jewish enemy :
cf. Matt. v. 44.

8. gift. In other words a 'bribe.'

10   And six years thou shalt sow thy land, and shalt gather
11 in the increase thereof: but the seventh year thou shalt
      let it rest and lie fallow ; that the poor of thy people may
      eat: and what they leave the beast of the field shall eat.
      In like manner thou shalt deal with thy vineyard, *and* with
12 thy oliveyard. Six days thou shalt do thy work, and on the
      seventh day thou shalt rest: that thine ox and thine ass
      may have rest, and the son of thy handmaid, and the
13 stranger, may be refreshed And in all things that I have
      said unto you take ye heed : and make no mention of the
      name of other gods, neither let it be heard out of thy mouth.
14   Three times thou shalt keep a feast unto me in the year.
15 The feast of unleavened bread shalt thou keep: seven
      days thou shalt eat unleavened bread, as I commanded
      thee, at the time appointed in the month Abib (for in it
      thou camest out from Egypt); and none shall appear be-
16 fore me empty: and the feast of harvest, the firstfruits of
      thy labours, which thou sowest in the field: and the feast

---

11. seventh. It is not certain whether the fallow year was to
be observed by all Israel at the same time (as in Lev. xxv. 1–7).
The most convenient way would be to let one-seventh of the land
lie fallow every year.

13. the name, etc. 'At a later time this prohibition led to
the practice of altering proper names compounded with Baal,
e.g. Ish-*bosheth* for Ish-*baal*, etc.' (McNeile).

14. Three times, etc. According to the opinion of most recent
scholars all three festivals are agricultural in origin. Later tradition attached them to certain historic events.

15. The feast of unleavened bread. Better 'cakes.' This festival was held to celebrate the beginning of barley-harvest ; its
origin is unknown. In xii. 14 ff., xiii. 3 ff. there is a historical
connexion with the exodus.

16. the feast of harvest. To celebrate the end of wheat
harvest. This festival is elsewhere called the feast of weeks; see
xxxiv. 22. It was held by the later Jews to commemorate the
giving of the law, and from being celebrated on the fiftieth day
after the Passover acquired the name of Pentecost.

the feast of ingathering=the feast of booths or tabernacles.
To commemorate the fruit harvest.

of ingathering, at the end of the year, when thou gatherest in thy labours out of the field. Three times in the year all 17 thy males shall appear before the Lord GOD.

Thou shalt not offer the blood of my sacrifice with 18 leavened bread; neither shall the fat of my feast remain all night until the morning. The first of the firstfruits of 19 thy ground thou shalt bring into the house of the LORD thy God. Thou shalt not seethe a kid in its mother's milk.

xxiii. 20–33. *Exhortation to obedience.*

Behold, I send an angel before thee, to keep thee by 20 the way, and to bring thee into the place which I have prepared. Take ye heed of him, and hearken unto his 21 voice; provoke him not: for he will not pardon your transgression; for my name is in him. But if thou shalt indeed 22 hearken unto his voice, and do all that I speak; then I will be an enemy unto thine enemies, and an adversary unto thine adversaries. For mine angel shall go before 23 thee, and bring thee in unto the Amorite, and the Hittite, and the Perizzite, and the Canaanite, the Hivite, and the Jebusite: and I will cut them off. Thou shalt not bow 24 down to their gods, nor serve them, nor do after their works: but thou shalt utterly overthrow them, and break in pieces their pillars. And ye shall serve the LORD your God, and 25 he shall bless thy bread, and thy water; and I will take sickness away from the midst of thee. There shall none 26

---

16. end of the year. See on xii. 2.

19. seethe a kid, etc. Again in xxxiv. 26; Deut. xiv. 21. The origin of this prohibition seems to be to prevent some kind of magic rite: cf. Frazer, *Folk-Lore in O.T.* III. pp. 111 ff.

20. an angel. Cf. iii. 2; Numb. x. 31 ff.

24. pillars. These stones were erected near an altar or temple. Primitive people believed that the deity actually inhabited them: cf. Driver on Gen. xxviii. 18.

25. sickness. Cf. the similar though more restricted promise of xv. 26.

cast her young, nor be barren, in thy land : the number of
27 thy days I will fulfil. I will send my terror before thee, and
will discomfit all the people to whom thou shalt come, and
I will make all thine enemies turn their backs unto thee.
28 And I will send the hornet before thee, which shall drive
out the Hivite, the Canaanite, and the Hittite, from before
29 thee. I will not drive them out from before thee in one
year ; lest the land become desolate, and the beast of the
30 field multiply against thee. By little and little I will drive
them out from before thee, until thou be increased, and
31 inherit the land. And I will set thy border from the Red
Sea even unto the sea of the Philistines, and from the
wilderness unto the River : for I will deliver the inhabitants
of the land into your hand ; and thou shalt drive them out
32 before thee. Thou shalt make no covenant with them, nor
33 with their gods. They shall not dwell in thy land, lest they
make thee sin against me : for if thou serve their gods, it
will surely be a snare unto thee.

xxiv. 1–11. *The vision of Jehovah.*

24 And he said unto Moses, Come up unto the LORD, thou,
and Aaron, Nadab, and Abihu, and seventy of the elders

28. the hornet. This plague of hornets is evidently intended
to be taken literally : cf. Deut. vii. 20; Jos. xxiv. 12.
the Hivite, etc. See on iii. 8.
29. lest the land, etc. Cf. Tennyson's description of the
effects of the Saxon invasion of Britain in *The Coming of
Arthur*, 10 ff. :

'So there grew great tracts of wilderness,
Wherein the beast was ever more and more,
But man was less and less, till Arthur came.'

30. little and little. Two different conceptions of the occu-
pation of Canaan evidently existed in Israel ; one regarded the
conquest as slow and gradual (here, Deut. vii. 22; Jos. xiii. 13;
Jud. i. 19, etc.), the other as rapid and immediate (Jos. x. 28 ff.,
xi. 16 ff., etc.).
31. The ideal borders of Israel : cf. 1 Kings iv. 21.
the River. The Euphrates.
xxiv. 1. Nadab, and Abihu. Sons of Aaron (xxviii. 1), de-

of Israel; and worship ye afar off: and Moses alone shall 2
come near unto the LORD; but they shall not come near;
neither shall the people go up with him. And Moses came 3
and told the people all the words of the LORD, and all the
judgements: and all the people answered with one voice,
and said, All the words which the LORD hath spoken will
we do. And Moses wrote all the words of the LORD, 4
and rose up early in the morning, and builded an altar
under the mount, and twelve pillars, according to the twelve
tribes of Israel. And he sent young men of the children of 5
Israel, which offered burnt offerings, and sacrificed peace
offerings of oxen unto the LORD. And Moses took half of 6
the blood, and put it in basons; and half of the blood he
sprinkled on the altar. And he took the book of the cove- 7
nant, and read in the audience of the people: and they
said, All that the LORD hath spoken will we do, and be
obedient. And Moses took the blood, and sprinkled it on 8
the people, and said, Behold the blood of the covenant,
which the LORD hath made with you concerning all these
words. Then went up Moses, and Aaron, Nadab, and 9
Abihu, and seventy of the elders of Israel: and they saw 10

---

stroyed for offering 'strange fire' to Jehovah (Lev. x. 1 ff.). In
spite of the great privilege here afforded them they fell into sin;
they 'see under His feet the body of heaven in its clearness, yet
go down to kindle the censer against their own souls' (Ruskin).

4. pillars. See on xxiii. 24. Notice that Moses here erects
these 'standing stones' which later are forbidden (Lev. xxvi. 1;
Deut. xvi. 22).

5. young men. There is no mention here of Levites.

burnt offerings...peace offerings. See on xx. 24.

7. the book of the covenant. This contained xx. 22–xxiii. 33,
though probably omissions should be made.

they said, etc In ancient times, as at the present, the popu-
lar reception of a law was exceedingly important. Cf. Stubbs,
Constitutional History, I. p. 130.

8. the blood of the covenant. Cf. Mark xiv. 24; Matt.
xxvi. 28.

10. they saw, etc. In the cloudless sky the glory of God

the God of Israel; and there was under his feet as it were
a paved work of sapphire stone, and as it were the very
11 heaven for clearness. And upon the nobles of the children
of Israel he laid not his hand: and they beheld God, and
did eat and drink.

12–18. *Moses goes up into the mount.*

12   And the LORD said unto Moses, Come up to me into
the mount, and be there : and I will give thee the tables
of stone, and the law and the commandment, which I have
13 written, that thou mayest teach them. And Moses rose up,
and Joshua his minister : and Moses went up into the mount
14 of God. And he said unto the elders, Tarry ye here for us,
until we come again unto you : and, behold, Aaron and
Hur are with you: whosoever hath a cause, let him come
15 near unto them. And Moses went up into the mount, and
16 the cloud covered the mount. And the glory of the LORD
abode upon mount Sinai, and the cloud covered it six days :
and the seventh day he called unto Moses out of the midst
17 of the cloud. And the appearance of the glory of the LORD
was like devouring fire on the top of the mount in the eyes
18 of the children of Israel. And Moses entered into the midst
of the cloud, and went up into the mount: and Moses was
in the mount forty days and forty nights.

---

appeared. In view of John i. 18, 'No man hath seen God at
any time,' the statement cannot be taken literally : LXX guards
against this by paraphrasing.
   12. tables of stone. This is the expression used in E. J and
Deut. refer to 'the two tables of stone*s*' (xxxiv. 1, 4; Deut. iv.
13, v. 22, etc.). In P the phrase is 'the two tables of the testimony' (xxxi. 18 a, xxxii. 15 a, etc.).
   16. the glory of the LORD. The visible manifestation of God's
presence : cf. xl. 34 f. This appearance is usually connected, as
here, with a glowing light, a fiery cloud : cf. Numb. xiv. 10,
xvi. 19, etc.
   18. forty days and forty nights: cf. Matt. iv. 2. 'The space
of forty days is always in Scripture a period of solemn waiting
followed by issues of momentous interest' (Westcott).

xxv. 1–9. *The offerings for the sanctuary.*

And the LORD spake unto Moses, saying, Speak unto 25 2
the children of Israel, that they take for me an offering: of
every man whose heart maketh him willing ye shall take
my offering. And this is the offering which ye shall take 3
of them; gold, and silver, and brass; and blue, and purple, 4
and scarlet, and fine linen, and goats' *hair*; and rams' skins 5
dyed red, and sealskins, and acacia wood; oil for the light, 6
spices for the anointing oil, and for the sweet incense;
onyx stones, and stones to be set, for the ephod, and for 7
the breastplate. And let them make me a sanctuary; that 8
I may dwell among them. According to all that I shew 9
thee, the pattern of the tabernacle, and the pattern of all
the furniture thereof, even so shall ye make it.

---

xxv. 2. offering. Lit. 'something taken off'; LXX ἀφαίρεμα.

3. brass. Strictly speaking brass, which is an alloy of copper
and zinc, was unknown in ancient times. 'Copper' or 'bronze'
(i.e. copper and tin) is a better translation.

4. blue, better 'hyacinth' or 'violet.' This colour, like that
which follows, was obtained from a shellfish. Philo and Josephus
explain that it signifies the sky.

purple. The old 'purple' was a dark red.

scarlet. This dye came from an insect found on the leaves of
the oak. The Arabs call it *ḳirmiz*, from which our word 'crim-
son' is derived.

5. sealskins. The meaning of the original word *taḥash* is
unknown: some connect it with an Egyptian word *tḥs* = leather.
The Arabic *tuḥas*, however, = dolphin, so perhaps some marine
animal is referred to.

7. ephod...breastplate. Described in xxviii. 6 ff.; see notes
there.

9. tabernacle. Better 'dwelling.' Two entirely different conceptions of this structure seem to be found in JE and P respec-
tively. The former is much less elaborate: cf. xxxiii. 7 ff.; Numb.
xi. 16 ff.; Deut. xxxi. 14 f., with the various passages of P, such
as the present series of chh. xxv.–xxvii. or Numb. ii., etc.

10-22. *The ark and the cherubim.*

10 And they shall make an ark of acacia wood : two cubits
and a half shall be the length thereof, and a cubit and a
half the breadth thereof, and a cubit and a half the height
11 thereof. And thou shalt overlay it with pure gold, within
and without shalt thou overlay it, and shalt make upon it
12 a crown of gold round about. And thou shalt cast four
rings of gold for it, and put them in the four feet thereof ;
and two rings shall be on the one side of it, and two rings
13 on the other side of it. And thou shalt make staves of
14 acacia wood, and overlay them with gold. And thou shalt
put the staves into the rings on the sides of the ark, to bear
15 the ark withal. The staves shall be in the rings of the ark :
16 they shall not be taken from it. And thou shalt put into
17 the ark the testimony which I shall give thee. And thou
shalt make a mercy-seat of pure gold : two cubits and a
half *shall be* the length thereof, and a cubit and a half the
18 breadth thereof. And thou shalt make two cherubim of
gold ; of beaten work shalt thou make them, at the two
19 ends of the mercy-seat. And make one cherub at the one

---

10. an ark. A box or chest ; for its history see McNeile,
pp. 161 ff.

cubit=about 1 ft. 6 in.

15. not be taken from it. Contrast Numb. iv. 6.

16. the testimony. Referring to the Decalogue, though the
term has also a wider connotation (Ps. xix. 7, cxix. 88, etc.).

17. mercy-seat. The Heb. root which underlies the word
means 'to propitiate.' This mercy-seat 'was to the Jew the
most sacred spot on earth ; Yahweh appeared there attended by
adoring cherubim ; and there the high priest on the Day of
Atonement presented the blood by which the sins of the nation
were..."wiped away"' (McNeile).

18. cherubim. These first appear in Gen. iii. 24, where they
are appointed to guard the gate of Eden ; their other function
was to bear Jehovah (Ps. xviii. 10, etc.). The conception of these
winged human figures is doubtless mythological, as they are found
widely amongst primitive peoples ; e.g. Aeschylus, *Prom. Vinct.*
803 f. ; Herodotus, III. 116, etc.

end, and one cherub at the other end: of one piece with the mercy-seat shall ye make the cherubim on the two ends thereof. And the cherubim shall spread out their wings 20 on high, covering the mercy-seat with their wings, with their faces one to another; toward the mercy-seat shall the faces of the cherubim be. And thou shalt put the mercy- 21 seat above upon the ark; and in the ark thou shalt put the testimony that I shall give thee. And there I will meet 22 with thee, and I will commune with thee from above the mercy-seat, from between the two cherubim which are upon the ark of the testimony, of all things which I will give thee in commandment unto the children of Israel.

23–30. *The table of the presence-bread.*

And thou shalt make a table of acacia wood : two cubits 23 *shall be* the length thereof, and a cubit the breadth there‑ of, and a cubit and a half the height thereof. And thou 24 shalt overlay it with pure gold, and make thereto a crown of gold round about. And thou shalt make unto it a border 25 of an handbreadth round about, and thou shalt make a golden crown to the border thereof round about. And 26 thou shalt make for it four rings of gold, and put the rings in the four corners that are on the four feet thereof. Close by the border shall the rings be, for places for the 27 staves to bear the table. And thou shalt make the staves 28 of acacia wood, and overlay them with gold, that the table may be borne with them. And thou shalt make the dishes 29 thereof, and the spoons thereof, and the flagons thereof,

---

20. In Solomon's Temple the arrangement was different: 1 Kings vi. 23 ff.

22. I will meet. Hence the name, 'Tent of Meeting' or 'Tryst.' The position of Moses is superior to that of Aaron (cf. Lev. xvi. 2 ff.).

23. a table. The measurements, except for the width, were the same as those of the ark.

25. border, better 'rail.'

29. spoons, better, with LXX, 'incense-cups.'

and the bowls thereof, to pour out withal : of pure gold
30 shalt thou make them. And thou shalt set upon the table
shewbread before me alway.

31-40. *The golden lampstand.*

31   And thou shalt make a candlestick of pure gold : of
beaten work shall the candlestick be made, even its base,
and its shaft; its cups, its knops, and its flowers, shall be
32 of one piece with it : and there shall be six branches going
out of the sides thereof ; three branches of the candlestick
out of the one side thereof, and three branches of the
33 candlestick out of the other side thereof : three cups made
like almond-blossoms in one branch, a knop and a flower ;
and three cups made like almond-blossoms in the other
branch, a knop and a flower : so for the six branches going
34 out of the candlestick : and in the candlestick four cups
made like almond-blossoms, the knops thereof, and the
35 flowers thereof : and a knop under two branches of one
piece with it, and a knop under two branches of one piece
with it, and a knop under two branches of one piece with
36 it, for the six branches going out of the candlestick. Their
knops and their branches shall be of one piece with it : the
37 whole of it one beaten work of pure gold. And thou shalt
make the lamps thereof, seven : and they shall light the
38 lamps thereof, to give light over against it. And the tongs
thereof, and the snuffdishes thereof, shall be of pure gold.
39 Of a talent of pure gold shall it be made, with all these
40 vessels. And see that thou make them after their pattern,
which hath been shewed thee in the mount.

---

30. shewbread, better, with margin, ' Presence-bread.' The
original idea no doubt was that Jehovah needed food.

31. candlestick, better ' lampstand,' since lamps and not
candles were placed on it.

37. light, margin ' set up.' There can be but little doubt that
there is no reference here to lighting, but to placing the lighted
lamps in position on the stand.

39. a talent = 673,500 grs. or nearly 100 lbs. avoirdupois.

xxvi. 1–14. *The curtains of the tabernacle.*

Moreover thou shalt make the tabernacle with ten cur- 26
tains of fine twined linen, and blue, and purple, and scarlet,
with cherubim the work of the cunning workman shalt
thou make them. The length of each curtain shall be 2
eight and twenty cubits, and the breadth of each curtain
four cubits : all the curtains shall have one measure. Five 3
curtains shall be coupled together one to another ; and
the other five curtains shall be coupled one to another.
And thou shalt make loops of blue upon the edge of the 4
one curtain from the selvedge in the coupling ; and likewise shalt thou make in the edge of the curtain that is
outmost in the second coupling. Fifty loops shalt thou 5
make in the one curtain, and fifty loops shalt thou make
in the edge of the curtain that is in the second coupling ;
the loops shall be opposite one to another. And thou 6
shalt make fifty clasps of gold, and couple the curtains
one to another with the clasps : and the tabernacle shall
be one. And thou shalt make curtains of goats' *hair* for 7
a tent over the tabernacle : eleven curtains shalt thou
make them. The length of each curtain shall be thirty 8
cubits, and the breadth of each curtain four cubits : the
eleven curtains shall have one measure. And thou shalt 9
couple five curtains by themselves, and six curtains by
themselves, and shalt double over the sixth curtain in the
forefront of the tent. And thou shalt make fifty loops on 10
the edge of the one curtain that is outmost in the coupling,
and fifty loops upon the edge of the curtain which is *outmost in* the second coupling. And thou shalt make fifty 11
clasps of brass, and put the clasps into the loops, and

---

xxvi. 1. the tabernacle. Not here the whole structure (as in
xxv. 9, xl. 18, etc.), but only the Holy place and the Holy of
holies.

7. goats' hair. The material of an ordinary tent.

12 couple the tent together, that it may be one. And the
overhanging part that remaineth of the curtains of the
tent, the half curtain that remaineth shall hang over the
13 back of the tabernacle. And the cubit on the one side, and
the cubit on the other side, of that which remaineth in
the length of the curtains of the tent, shall hang over the
sides of the tabernacle on this side and on that side, to
14 cover it. And thou shalt make a covering for the tent of
rams' skins dyed red, and a covering of sealskins above.

15–30. *The woodwork.*

15 And thou shalt make the boards for the tabernacle of
16 acacia wood, standing up. Ten cubits shall be the length
of a board, and a cubit and a half the breadth of each
17 board. Two tenons shall there be in each board, joined
one to another: thus shalt thou make for all the boards of
18 the tabernacle. And thou shalt make the boards for the
tabernacle, twenty boards for the south side southward.
19 And thou shalt make forty sockets of silver under the
twenty boards; two sockets under one board for its two
tenons, and two sockets under another board for its two
20 tenons: and for the second side of the tabernacle, on the
north side, twenty boards: and their forty sockets of
21 silver; two sockets under one board, and two sockets
22 under another board. And for the hinder part of the
23 tabernacle westward thou shalt make six boards. And two

---

12. This cannot be reconciled with *v.* 9 and may be a gloss.
15. boards. Better 'frames.'
17. tenons. The uprights of which each frame was composed.
18. south side. Heb. *negeb*; from the arid district lying to the south of Judah.
19. sockets. Better 'bases' or 'pedestals.'
22. westward. Lit. 'towards the sea.' This expression, like that in *v.* 18, must have arisen amongst a people long dwelling in Canaan.

boards shalt thou make for the corners of the tabernacle
in the hinder part. And they shall be double beneath, and 24
in like manner they shall be entire unto the top thereof
unto one ring: thus shall it be for them both; they shall
be for the two corners. And there shall be eight boards, 25
and their sockets of silver, sixteen sockets; two sockets
under one board, and two sockets under another board.
And thou shalt make bars of acacia wood; five for the 26
boards of the one side of the tabernacle, and five bars for 27
the boards of the other side of the tabernacle, and five
bars for the boards of the side of the tabernacle, for the
hinder part westward. And the middle bar in the midst of 28
the boards shall pass through from end to end. And thou 29
shalt overlay the boards with gold, and make their rings
of gold for places for the bars: and thou shalt overlay the
bars with gold. And thou shalt rear up the tabernacle 30
according to the fashion thereof which hath been shewed
thee in the mount.

31-37. *The veil and the screen.*

And thou shalt make a veil of blue, and purple, and 31
scarlet, and fine twined linen: with cherubim the work of
the cunning workman shall it be made: and thou shalt 32
hang it upon four pillars of acacia overlaid with gold, their
hooks *shall be* of gold, upon four sockets of silver. And 33
thou shalt hang up the veil under the clasps, and shalt
bring in thither within the veil the ark of the testimony:
and the veil shall divide unto you between the holy place
and the most holy. And thou shalt put the mercy-seat 34
upon the ark of the testimony in the most holy place. And 35

---

24. This verse cannot really be understood and no suggested
scheme is quite satisfactory: see Driver, p. 288; McNeile,
pp. lxxv f.; and cf. the various suggestions in regard to the
bridge described by Caesar in *De Bell. Gall.* IV. 17.
31. a veil. Cf. Heb. ix. 7 f., x. 19 ff.

thou shalt set the table without the veil, and the candlestick over against the table on the side of the tabernacle
toward the south: and thou shalt put the table on the
36 north side. And thou shalt make a screen for the door of
the Tent, of blue, and purple, and scarlet, and fine twined
37 linen, the work of the embroiderer. And thou shalt make
for the screen five pillars of acacia, and overlay them with
gold; their hooks shall be of gold: and thou shalt cast
five sockets of brass for them.

xxvii. 1–8. *The altar of burnt offering.*

27   And thou shalt make the altar of acacia wood, five cubits
long, and five cubits broad; the altar shall be foursquare:
2 and the height thereof shall be three cubits. And thou
shalt make the horns of it upon the four corners thereof:
the horns thereof shall be of one piece with it: and thou
3 shalt overlay it with brass. And thou shalt make its pots
to take away its ashes, and its shovels, and its basons, and
its fleshhooks, and its firepans: all the vessels thereof
4 thou shalt make of brass. And thou shalt make for it a
grating of network of brass; and upon the net shalt thou
5 make four brasen rings in the four corners thereof. And
thou shalt put it under the ledge round the altar beneath,
6 that the net may reach halfway up the altar. And thou
shalt make staves for the altar, staves of acacia wood, and
7 overlay them with brass. And the staves thereof shall be

---

xxvii. 1. the altar. Cf. xxx. 1, *an* altar.

foursquare, i.e. 'with four equal sides.'

2. the horns. The origin of the custom of having horned
altars is obscure, though such altars are found amongst the
Assyrians and Greeks. Some think they arose from placing the
horns of the victims on the altar, and that later a conventional
symbol was used. The horns were an important part of the
altar: cf. xxix. 12; 1 Kings i. 50; Jer. xvii. 1.

5. the ledge. In order that the priests should be able to reach
to the top of the altar they would require a step or ledge on
which to stand.

put into the rings, and the staves shall be upon the two sides of the altar, in bearing it. Hollow with planks shalt 8 thou make it : as it hath been shewed thee in the mount, so shall they make it.

9-19. *The court of the tabernacle.*

And thou shalt make the court of the tabernacle : for 9 the south side southward there shall be hangings for the court of fine twined linen an hundred cubits long for one side : and the pillars thereof shall be twenty, and their 10 sockets twenty, of brass ; the hooks of the pillars and their fillets *shall be* of silver. And likewise for the north side in 11 length there shall be hangings an hundred cubits long, and the pillars thereof twenty, and their sockets twenty, of brass ; the hooks of the pillars and their fillets of silver. And for the breadth of the court on the west side shall be 12 hangings of fifty cubits : their pillars ten, and their sockets ten. And the breadth of the court on the east side east- 13 ward shall be fifty cubits. The hangings for the one side 14 *of the gate* shall be fifteen cubits : their pillars three, and their sockets three. And for the other side shall be hang- 15 ings of fifteen cubits : their pillars three, and their sockets three. And for the gate of the court shall be a screen of 16 twenty cubits, of blue, and purple, and scarlet, and fine twined linen, the work of the embroiderer : their pillars four, and their sockets four. All the pillars of the court 17

---

8. Hollow with planks. ' Wishing to picture a portable altar the narrator disregarded its practical inutility. A hot fire burning within it would soon have destroyed it ' (McNeile). Some think an earthen or stone altar was put inside : cf. xx. 24 f.

9. the court. This legislation makes no provision for a special court for the priests : cf. Ezek. xl. 17 ff.; 1 Macc. iv. 38, 48.

10. their fillets. The word is usually applied to a headband or ribbon; here it probably means ' a band of silver at the base of the capital.' Some would translate ' connecting-rods,' but this has not much to commend it.

round about shall be filleted with silver ; their hooks of
18 silver, and their sockets of brass. The length of the court
shall be an hundred cubits, and the breadth fifty every
where, and the height five cubits, of fine twined linen, and
19 their sockets of brass. All the instruments of the tabernacle in all the service thereof, and all the pins thereof,
and all the pins of the court, shallbe of brass.

20 f. *Oil for the lamp.*

20   And thou shalt command the children of Israel, that
they bring unto thee pure olive oil beaten for the light, to
21 cause a lamp to burn continually. In the tent of meeting,
without the veil which is before the testimony, Aaron and
his sons shall order it from evening to morning before the
LORD : it shall be a statute for ever throughout their
generations on the behalf of the children of Israel.

xxviii. 1–5. *The priestly vestments.*

28   And bring thou near unto thee Aaron thy brother, and
his sons with him, from among the children of Israel, that

---

18. every where. The text is here corrupt. The Samaritan
reads 'cubits.'

20. they bring unto thee. The supply of oil is regarded as
an important matter: so too in the early days of the Church at
Rome certain estates were set aside as a provision for the supply
of oil and lamps: see Spearing, *The Patrimony of the Roman
Church*, p. 12.

beaten. The olives were crushed in a mortar and the pulp
was strained so that the liquid was separated.

continually. So Lev. xxiv. 2. It must not be supposed, however, that the lamps were never allowed to go out like the fire in
the Temple of Vesta ('ignem illum Vestae sempiternum,' as Cicero
calls it, *In Cat.* IV. 18) : cf. xxx. 8; 1 Sam. iii. 3. 'Regularly'
is meant, not 'uninterruptedly.'

21. the tent of meeting. The oldest name for the Tabernacle.
It occurs in both JE and P, though not perhaps with the same
meaning: see xxxiii. 7; Numb. xi. 16; Deut. xxxi. 14 (JE):
xv. 22, xxx. 6, 26 (P).

xxviii. 1. Aaron...and his sons. This notice anticipates chs.
xxviii.–xxix.

he may minister unto me in the priest's office, even Aaron,
Nadab and Abihu, Eleazar and Ithamar, Aaron's sons.
And thou shalt make holy garments for Aaron thy brother, 2
for glory and for beauty.   And thou shalt speak unto all 3
that are wise hearted, whom I have filled with the spirit
of wisdom, that they make Aaron's garments to sanctify
him, that he may minister unto me in the priest's office.
And these are the garments which they shall make; a 4
breastplate, and an ephod, and a robe, and a coat of chequer
work, a mitre, and a girdle : and they shall make holy
garments for Aaron thy brother, and his sons, that he may
minister unto me in the priest's office.   And they shall 5
take the gold, and the blue, and the purple, and the scarlet,
and the fine linen.

6-12. *The golden ephod.*

And they shall make the ephod of gold, of blue, and 6
purple, scarlet, and fine twined linen, the work of the
cunning workman.   It shall have two shoulderpieces joined 7
to the two ends thereof; that it may be joined together.
And the cunningly woven band, which is upon it, to gird 8
it on withal, shall be like the work thereof *and* of the
same piece ; of gold, of blue, and purple, and scarlet, and
fine twined linen.   And thou shalt take two onyx stones, 9
and grave on them the names of the children of Israel :

---

1. Nadab and Abihu. Mentioned above, vi. 23 (P) and xxxiv.
1 (J).
Eleazar and Ithamar. Eleazar is the more prominent of this
pair of Aaron's sons and later succeeded his father (Numb. xx. 26;
Deut. x. 6). Ithamar appears in xxxviii. 21; Numb. iv. 28, 33, etc.
3. I have filled. The Holy Spirit is the source of all gifts,
not only of those which we call 'spiritual.'
6. ephod. The ephod was a decorated garment worn by the
High Priest and supported by shoulder-straps.   Some scholars
think that the ephod came below the waist and was a kind of
kilt, others that it was worn above more like a waistcoat without
an opening in the front.

10 six of their names on the one stone, and the names of the
   six that remain on the other stone, according to their
11 birth. With the work of an engraver in stone, like the
   engravings of a signet, shalt thou engrave the two stones,
   according to the names of the children of Israel: thou
12 shalt make them to be inclosed in ouches of gold. And
   thou shalt put the two stones upon the shoulderpieces of
   the ephod, to be stones of memorial for the children of
   Israel: and Aaron shall bear their names before the LORD
   upon his two shoulders for a memorial.

13–30. *The breastplate of judgement.*

13 And thou shalt make ouches of gold: and two chains of
14 pure gold; like cords shalt thou make them, of wreathen
   work: and thou shalt put the wreathen chains on the
15 ouches. And thou shalt make a breastplate of judgement,
   the work of the cunning workman; like the work of the
   ephod thou shalt make it; of gold, of blue, and purple,
   and scarlet, and fine twined linen, shalt thou make it.
16 Foursquare it shall be *and* double; a span shall be the
17 length thereof, and a span the breadth thereof. And
   thou shalt set in it settings of stones, four rows of stones:
   a row of sardius, topaz, and carbuncle shall be the first

---

11. ouches. Better 'rosettes' (LXX ἀσπιδίσκαι).

12. a memorial. The names are also carried on Aaron's heart
by being inscribed on the breastplate (*v.* 29): in both cases to
keep them in the mind of Jehovah.

15. breastplate. This translation seems to be a guess: 'pouch'
suits the context better (cf. *v.* 30).

of judgement. So called because containing the Urim and
Thummim (*vv.* 29 f.).

17–20. Lists of precious stones are also found in xxxix. 10 ff.;
Ezek. xxviii. 13; Rev. xxi. 19 f. The identification of the stones
is far from certain and the renderings in LXX and other versions
do not greatly help.

17. sardius. Heb. = redness, the stone may be the cornelian.
topaz. Probably a chrysolite: see 'beryl,' (*v.* 20).
carbuncle. A rock-crystal; used by Nero for an eye-glass
(Pliny, *Hist. Nat.* XXXVII. 64).

row; and the second row an emerald, a sapphire, and a 18
diamond; and the third row a jacint, an agate, and an 19
amethyst; and the fourth row a beryl, and an onyx, and a 20
jasper: they shall be inclosed in gold in their settings.
And the stones shall be according to the names of the 21
children of Israel, twelve, according to their names; like
the engravings of a signet, every one according to his
name, they shall be for the twelve tribes. And thou shalt 22
make upon the breastplate chains like cords, of wreathen
work of pure gold. And thou shalt make upon the breast- 23
plate two rings of gold, and shalt put the two rings on the
two ends of the breastplate. And thou shalt put the two 24
wreathen chains of gold on the two rings at the ends of
the breastplate. And the *other* two ends of the two wreathen 25
chains thou shalt put on the two ouches, and put them on
the shoulderpieces of the ephod, in the forepart thereof.
And thou shalt make two rings of gold, and thou shalt put 26
them upon the two ends of the breastplate, upon the edge
thereof, which is toward the side of the ephod inward.
And thou shalt make two rings of gold, and shalt put them 27
on the two shoulderpieces of the ephod underneath, in the
forepart thereof, close by the coupling thereof, above the
cunningly woven band of the ephod. And they shall bind 28
the breastplate by the rings thereof unto the rings of the
ephod with a lace of blue, that it may be upon the cunningly woven band of the ephod, and that the breastplate
be not loosed from the ephod. And Aaron shall bear the 29
names of the children of Israel in the breastplate of judgement upon his heart, when he goeth in unto the holy place,

---

18. emerald. Probably the red garnet.

sapphire. Since our sapphire was not known till later times
the blue lapis lazuli is almost certainly meant.

diamond. The marg. 'sardonyx' is better: diamonds were
hardly known so early.

19. jacint. Perhaps the cairngorm.

20. beryl. Probably the modern topaz.

30 for a memorial before the LORD continually. And thou
shalt put in the breastplate of judgement the Urim and the
Thummim; and they shall be upon Aaron's heart, when
he goeth in before the LORD: and Aaron shall bear the
judgement of the children of Israel upon his heart before
the LORD continually.

31–35. *The robe of the ephod.*

31   And thou shalt make the robe of the ephod all of blue.
32 And it shall have a hole for the head in the midst thereof:
it shall have a binding of woven work round about the
hole of it, as it were the hole of a coat of mail, that it be
33 not rent. And upon the skirts of it thou shalt make pomegranates of blue, and of purple, and of scarlet, round about
the skirts thereof; and bells of gold between them round
34 about : a golden bell and a pomegranate, a golden bell
and a pomegranate, upon the skirts of the robe round
35 about. And it shall be upon Aaron to minister : and the
sound thereof shall be heard when he goeth in unto the
holy place before the LORD, and when he cometh out, that
he die not.

36–39. *The high-priest's mitre.*

36   And thou shalt make a plate of puré gold, and grave
upon it, like the engravings of a signet, HOLY TO THE

---

29. a memorial. See on *v.* 12.
30. the Urim and the Thummim. Almost certainly two stones
used in divination. In 1 Sam. xiv. 41 (LXX) *Urim* was to be
given if the guilt lay with Saul or his house, *Thummim* if with
the people; see further, McNeile, pp. 182 ff.; Driver, pp. 313 f.
32. coat of mail. Better a 'linen corselet.' McNeile com-
pares λινοθώρηξ of *Iliad*, II. 529, 830.
33. pomegranates...bells. Flinders Petrie suggests that these
ornaments were borrowed from the lotus and bud pattern of the
Egyptians.
35. that he die not. Some danger evidently threatened
Aaron if he went in without the bells, perhaps from evil spirits :
see Frazer, *Folk-Lore in O.T.* III. pp. 446 ff.
36. a plate. Lit. 'a shining thing.'
HOLY TO THE LORD. Cf. Zech. xiv. 20.

LORD. And thou shalt put it on a lace of blue, and it shall 37
be upon the mitre; upon the forefront of the mitre it shall
be. And it shall be upon Aaron's forehead, and Aaron 38
shall bear the iniquity of the holy things, which the children
of Israel shall hallow in all their holy gifts; and it shall
be always upon his forehead, that they may be accepted
before the LORD. And thou shalt weave the coat in chequer 39
work of fine linen, and thou shalt make a mitre of fine
linen, and thou shalt make a girdle, the work of the embroiderer.

40–43. *Vestments for the priests.*

And for Aaron's sons thou shalt make coats, and thou 40
shalt make for them girdles, and headtires shalt thou
make for them, for glory and for beauty. And thou shalt 41
put them upon Aaron thy brother, and upon his sons with
him; and shalt anoint them, and consecrate them, and
sanctify them, that they may minister unto me in the
priest's office. And thou shalt make them linen breeches 42
to cover the flesh of their nakedness; from the loins even
unto the thighs they shall reach: and they shall be upon 43
Aaron, and upon his sons, when they go in unto the tent
of meeting, or when they come near unto the altar to
minister in the holy place; that they bear not iniquity, and
die: it shall be a statute for ever unto him and unto his
seed after him.

---

37. mitre. The marg. 'turban' is more in accordance with
the use of the word elsewhere: Isa. iii. 23 (of women), lxii. 3 (of
royalty), etc.
39. the coat. This is hardly a suitable name for the garment
which, according to Josephus, was close-fitting and reached to
the feet; 'cassock' would be better, or 'tunic.'
41. consecrate them: lit. 'fill their hand.' Perhaps the
priest was installed by having the sacrifice placed in his hands:
cf. xxix. 24.

xxix. 1-37. *The consecration of the priests.*

29   And this is the thing that thou shalt do unto them to
hallow them, to minister unto me in the priest's office:
take one young bullock and two rams without blemish,
2 and unleavened bread, and cakes unleavened mingled
with oil, and wafers unleavened anointed with oil: of
3 fine wheaten flour shalt thou make them. And thou
shalt put them into one basket, and bring them in the
4 basket, with the bullock and the two rams. And Aaron
and his sons thou shalt bring unto the door of the tent of
5 meeting, and shalt wash them with water. And thou shalt
take the garments, and put upon Aaron the coat, and the
robe of the ephod, and the ephod, and the breastplate, and
gird him with the cunningly woven band of the ephod:
6 and thou shalt set the mitre upon his head, and put the
7 holy crown upon the mitre. Then shalt thou take the
anointing oil, and pour it upon his head, and anoint him.
8 And thou shalt bring his sons, and put coats upon them.
9 And thou shalt gird them with girdles, Aaron and his
sons, and bind headtires on them: and they shall have
the priesthood by a perpetual statute: and thou shalt con-
10 secrate Aaron and his sons. And thou shalt bring the
bullock before the tent of meeting: and Aaron and his
sons shall lay their hands upon the head of the bullock.

xxix. 4. wash them. The whole person was cleansed: sub-
sequently the hands and feet had to be cleansed before the per-
formance of the daily office (xxx. 19 f.). This distinction may
have been in our Lord's mind in the incident of John xiii. 6-11.
   7. the anointing oil. See xxx. 22 ff. for its component parts;
and cf. Ps. cxxxiii. 2.
   anoint him. The high-priest only, as in *v.* 29, Lev. viii. 12.
In xxviii. 41, xxx. 30, etc., all the priests are anointed.
   9. consecrate. See on xxviii. 41.
   10. lay their hands. The traditional view held that this rite
caused the animal to become a substitute for the worshipper;
this view has now been abandoned by scholars (see Kennedy in
Hastings' *Dict. of the Bible* (1909), pp. 817 f.). All that was intended was to shew formally who was making the offering.

And thou shalt kill the bullock before the LORD, at the 11
door of the tent of meeting. And thou shalt take of the 12
blood of the bullock, and put it upon the horns of the altar
with thy finger; and thou shalt pour out all the blood at
the base of the altar. And thou shalt take all the fat that 13
covereth the inwards, and the caul upon the liver, and the
two kidneys, and the fat that is upon them, and burn them
upon the altar. But the flesh of the bullock, and its skin, 14
and its dung, shalt thou burn with fire without the camp:
it is a sin offering. Thou shalt also take the one ram; and 15
Aaron and his sons shall lay their hands upon the head of
the ram. And thou shalt slay the ram, and thou shalt take 16
its blood, and sprinkle it round about upon the altar. And 17
thou shalt cut the ram into its pieces, and wash its inwards,
and its legs, and put them with its pieces, and with its
head. And thou shalt burn the whole ram upon the altar: 18
it is a burnt offering unto the LORD: it is a sweet savour,
an offering made by fire unto the LORD. And thou shalt take 19
the other ram; and Aaron and his sons shall lay their
hands upon the head of the ram. Then shalt thou kill the 20
ram, and take of its blood, and put it upon the tip of the

---

12. horns. See on xxvii. 2.
of the altar. Cf. Lev. viii. 15.
13. the fat, etc. See more fully Lev. iii. 4, iv. 8 f. The *liver*
played an important part in certain modes of divination.
14. sin offering. Found only in 2 Kings xii. 16 before the exile
where it takes the form of a money payment: cf. Ezek. xl. 39,
xlii. 13.
16. sprinkle...upon. More correctly, 'throw against.'
18. a sweet savour: lit. 'an odour of rest-giving.' The term
comes down from very early days when the deity was thought to
enjoy the smell: cf. Gen. viii. 21.
20. The priest ' requires consecrated ears wherewith to understand the voice of God, consecrated hands because he performs
sacred functions, consecrated feet because he has to tread holy
ground' (Baentsch, following earlier commentators). When
Richard I was crowned the Archbishop anointed him on his head,
breast and arms, 'which signifies glory, valour, and knowledge':
see Roger de Hoveden, *Annals*, II. p. 118 (Bohn's edition).

right ear of Aaron, and upon the tip of the right ear of
his sons, and upon the thumb of their right hand, and
upon the great toe of their right foot, and sprinkle the
21 blood upon the altar round about. And thou shalt take of
the blood that is upon the altar, and of the anointing oil,
and sprinkle it upon Aaron, and upon his garments, and
upon his sons, and upon the garments of his sons with
him: and he shall be hallowed, and his garments, and his
22 sons, and his sons' garments with him. Also thou shalt
take of the ram the fat, and the fat tail, and the fat that
covereth the inwards, and the caul of the liver, and the two
kidneys, and the fat that is upon them, and the right thigh ;
23 for it is a ram of consecration : and one loaf of bread, and
one cake of oiled bread, and one wafer, out of the basket
24 of unleavened bread that is before the LORD : and thou
shalt put the whole upon the hands of Aaron, and upon
the hands of his sons; and shalt wave them for a wave
25 offering before the LORD. And thou shalt take them from
their hands, and burn them on the altar upon the burnt
offering, for a sweet savour before the LORD: it is an offer-
26 ing made by fire unto the LORD. And thou shalt take the
breast of Aaron's ram of consecration, and wave it for a
wave offering before the LORD : and it shall be thy portion.
27 And thou shalt sanctify the breast of the wave offering, and
the thigh of the heave offering, which is waved, and which
is heaved up, of the ram of consecration, even of that which
28 is for Aaron, and of that which is for his sons: and it shall
be for Aaron and his sons as a due for ever from the children of Israel: for it is an heave offering: and it shall be

---

21. **sprinkle.** A different word from that in *v.* 16.

24. **thou.** Moses himself is to consecrate Aaron and his sons.
upon the hands. That is the open palms : cf. Lev. viii. 27;
Numb. vi. 19.

28. **heave offering.** This does not mean that the offering was
elevated before Jehovah as the translation would suggest, but
that it was 'taken off' from the sacrifice for the priest.

an heave offering from the children of Israel of the sacrifices of their peace offerings, even their heave offering
unto the LORD. And the holy garments of Aaron shall be 29
for his sons after him, to be anointed in them, and to be
consecrated in them. Seven days shall the son that is 30
priest in his stead put them on, when he cometh into the
tent of meeting to minister in the holy place. And thou 31
shalt take the ram of consecration, and seethe its flesh in
a holy place. And Aaron and his sons shall eat the flesh 32
of the ram, and the bread that is in the basket, at the door
of the tent of meeting. And they shall eat those things 33
wherewith atonement was made, to consecrate *and* to
sanctify them: but a stranger shall not eat thereof, because
they are holy. And if aught of the flesh of the consecration, 34
or of the bread, remain unto the morning, then thou shalt
burn the remainder with fire: it shall not be eaten, because
it is holy. And thus shalt thou do unto Aaron, and to his 35
sons, according to all that I have commanded thee: seven
days shalt thou consecrate them. And every day shalt 36
thou offer the bullock of sin offering for atonement: and
thou shalt cleanse the altar, when thou makest atonement
for it; and thou shalt anoint it, to sanctify it. Seven days 37
thou shalt make atonement for the altar, and sanctify it:
and the altar shall be most holy; whatsoever toucheth the
altar shall be holy.

---

33. atonement. That is, 'reconciliation,' as always in the
Bible: 'the idea of *amends* or *reparation* for a fault, which the
word now mostly suggests, is not implied in either its Hebrew
or its Greek equivalent' (Driver).

stranger. To be distinguished from 'stranger' in xii. 48;
here=layman.

36. cleanse the altar: lit. 'un-sin the altar.' As sin to the
Hebrews was almost a physical thing, the nearest English equivalent would be 'disinfect': cf. Lev. xiv. 49.

37. holy. Holiness is contagious and those who touch a consecrated thing become 'taboo'; cf. xix. 12 f.

38-42. *The daily burnt offering.*

38 Now this is that which thou shalt offer upon the altar;
39 two lambs of the first year day by day continually. The
one lamb thou shalt offer in the morning; and the other
40 lamb thou shalt offer at even: and with the one lamb a
tenth part *of an ephah* of fine flour mingled with the fourth
part of an hin of beaten oil; and the fourth part of an hin
41 of wine for a drink offering. And the other lamb thou
shalt offer at even, and shalt do thereto according to the
meal offering of the morning, and according to the drink
offering thereof, for a sweet savour, an offering made by
42 fire unto the LORD. It shall be a continual burnt offering
throughout your generations at the door of the tent of
meeting before the LORD: where I will meet with you, to
speak there unto thee.

43-46. *Jehovah will dwell with His people.*

43 And there I will meet with the children of Israel; and
44 *the Tent* shall be sanctified by my glory. And I will sanctify the tent of meeting, and the altar: Aaron also and his
sons will I sanctify, to minister to me in the priest's office.
45 And I will dwell among the children of Israel, and will be
46 their God. And they shall know that I am the LORD their
God, that brought them forth out of the land of Egypt,
that I may dwell among them: I am the LORD their
God.

---

39. morning...even. In 2 Kings xvi. 15 the evening offering
is only cereal. Ezekiel seems to require no evening offering at
all (xlvi. 13 ff.). This law gives the post-exilic use (see Numb.
xxviii. 3 ff.).

40. the fourth part of an hin=about 2⅔ pints.

xxx. 1–10. *The altar of incense.*

And thou shalt make an altar to burn incense upon: of 30
acacia wood shalt thou make it. A cubit shall be the 2
length thereof, and a cubit the breadth thereof; foursquare
shall it be: and two cubits shall be the height thereof: the
horns thereof shall be of one piece with it. And thou shalt 3
overlay it with pure gold, the top thereof, and the sides
thereof round about, and the horns thereof; and thou
shalt make unto it a crown of gold round about. And two 4
golden rings shalt thou make for it under the crown thereof, upon the two ribs thereof, upon the two sides of it
shalt thou make them; and they shall be for places for
staves to bear it withal. And thou shalt make the staves 5
of acacia wood, and overlay them with gold. And thou 6
shalt put it before the veil that is by the ark of the testimony, before the mercy-seat that is over the testimony,
where I will meet with thee. And Aaron shall burn there- 7
on incense of sweet spices: every morning, when he
dresseth the lamps, he shall burn it. And when Aaron 8
lighteth the lamps at even, he shall burn it, a perpetual
incense before the LORD throughout your generations.
Ye shall offer no strange incense thereon, nor burnt offering, 9
nor meal offering; and ye shall pour no drink offering

---

xxx. 1. an altar...incense. This altar seems to be a later
addition as it is not mentioned in xxvi. 34 f. and the section deal-
ing with it is not at all suitable here (the Samaritan version places
vv. 1–13 after xxvi. 35). In Lev. x. and Numb. xvi. incense is
offered not on an altar but in censers. So too in xxvii. 1 only
one altar is recognised.
    incense: lit. 'sweet smoke.' The earliest mention of its use
in Israelite worship is probably Jer. vi. 20 (where see the present
writer's note).
    6. the testimony. See on xxv. 16.
    9. strange incense. Unauthorised, not made according to the
proper prescription, or by the proper persons.

10 thereon. And Aaron shall make atonement upon the horns
of it once in the year : with the blood of the sin offering of
atonement once in the year shall he make atonement for
it throughout your generations : it is most holy unto the
LORD.

11–16. *The tax of the half-shekel.*

11
12 And the LORD spake unto Moses, saying, When thou
takest the sum of the children of Israel, according to
those that are numbered of them, then shall they give
every man a ransom for his soul unto the LORD, when
thou numberest them; that there be no plague among
13 them, when thou numberest them. This they shall give,
every one that passeth over unto them that are numbered,
half a shekel after the shekel of the sanctuary : (the shekel
is twenty gerahs :) half a shekel for an offering to the
14 LORD. Every one that passeth over unto them that are
numbered, from twenty years old and upward, shall give
15 the offering of the LORD. The rich shall not give more,
and the poor shall not give less, than the half shekel, when
they give the offering of the LORD, to make atonement for

---

10. make atonement. The provision here is evidently intended to be a supplement to Lev. xvi. which makes no mention
of any altar of incense.

12. takest the sum. An anticipation of the census described
in Numb. i.

ransom. As in xxi. 30 (of a goring ox). There existed in
ancient times a widespread idea that numbering people or pos-
sessions was unlucky (2 Sam. xxiv.); here the payment seems to
be made to prevent the outbreak of a plague. See further, Frazer,
Folk-Lore in O.T. II. pp. 555 ff.

plague. In 2 Sam. xxiv. 15 a pestilence followed David's
census. If the present passage is later than the narrative in
2 Sam. xxiv.—as is almost certain—that event may account for
the warning here.

13. the shekel of the sanctuary. (LXX = the *holy* shekel.)
The silver shekel weighed 224 grains and was worth a little more
than 1*s*. in English money. This passage is the origin of the
Temple-tax of later times (cf. Matt. xvii. 24).

your souls. And thou shalt take the atonement money 16
from the children of Israel; and shalt appoint it for the
service of the tent of meeting; that it may be a memorial
for the children of Israel before the LORD, to make atonement for your souls.

17–21. *The bronze laver.*

And the LORD spake unto Moses, saying, Thou shalt 17
also make a laver of brass, and the base thereof of brass, 18
to wash withal: and thou shalt put it between the tent of
meeting and the altar, and thou shalt put water therein.
And Aaron and his sons shall wash their hands and their 19
feet thereat: when they go into the tent of meeting, they 20
shall wash with water, that they die not; or when they
come near to the altar to minister, to burn an offering
made by fire unto the LORD: so they shall wash their 21
hands and their feet, that they die not: and it shall be
a statute for ever to them, even to him and to his seed
throughout their generations.

22–38. *The composition of the oil and of the incense.*

Moreover the LORD spake unto Moses, saying, Take 22
thou also unto thee the chief spices, of flowing myrrh five 23
hundred *shekels*, and of sweet cinnamon half so much, even
two hundred and fifty, and of sweet calamus two hundred
and fifty, and of cassia five hundred, after the shekel of 24
the sanctuary, and of olive oil an hin: and thou shalt make 25
it an holy anointing oil, a perfume compounded after the
art of the perfumer: it shall be an holy anointing oil. And 26
thou shalt anoint therewith the tent of meeting, and the

---

16. for the service. Every Israelite, rich or poor, had to con-
tribute towards the maintenance of religious worship.
17. a laver. This article is not mentioned in the original in-
structions nor in Numb. iv. The laver served the same purpose
as the sacred lake which was attached to every Egyptian temple.
23. calamus. Better 'cane': cf. Jer. vi. 20.
24. cassia. The bark of a species of cinnamon tree.

27 ark of the testimony, and the table and all the vessels
thereof, and the candlestick and the vessels thereof, and
28 the altar of incense, and the altar of burnt offering with all
the vessels thereof, and the laver and the base thereof.
29 And thou shalt sanctify them, that they may be most holy:
30 whatsoever toucheth them shall be holy. And thou shalt
anoint Aaron and his sons, and sanctify them, that they
31 may minister unto me in the priest's office. And thou shalt
speak unto the children of Israel, saying, This shall be an
holy anointing oil unto me throughout your generations.
32 Upon the flesh of man shall it not be poured, neither shall
ye make any like it, according to the composition thereof:
33 it is holy, *and* it shall be holy unto you. Whosoever com-
poundeth any like it, or whosoever putteth any of it upon
a stranger, he shall be cut off from his people.

34 And the LORD said unto Moses, Take unto thee sweet
spices, stacte, and onycha, and galbanum; sweet spices
with pure frankincense: of each shall there be a like
35 weight; and thou shalt make of it incense, a perfume
after the art of the perfumer, seasoned with salt, pure *and*
36 holy: and thou shalt beat some of it very small, and put
of it before the testimony in the tent of meeting, where I
37 will meet with thee: it shall be unto you most holy. And
the incense which thou shalt make, according to the composition thereof ye shall not make for yourselves: it shall
38 be unto thee holy for the LORD. Whosoever shall make
like unto that, to smell thereto, he shall be cut off from his
people.

---

30. Aaron and his sons. In xxix. 7 the high-priest alone is to
be anointed.

34. stacte (=LXX στακτή). The kind of oil or resin here
meant is not certain; 'myrrh-oil' has been suggested as a possible rendering.

onycha. Still used amongst the Arabs.

galbanum. A species of resin.

35. with salt. This possibly had a symbolical value.

xxxi. 1–11. *The appointment of Bezalel and Oholiab.*

And the LORD spake unto Moses, saying, See, I have 31 2
called by name Bezalel the son of Uri, the son of Hur, of
the tribe of Judah: and I have filled him with the spirit of 3
God, in wisdom, and in understanding, and in knowledge,
and in all manner of workmanship, to devise cunning works, 4
to work in gold, and in silver, and in brass, and in cutting 5
of stones for setting, and in carving of wood, to work in all
manner of workmanship. And I, behold, I have appointed 6
with him Oholiab, the son of Ahisamach, of the tribe of
Dan; and in the hearts of all that are wise hearted I have
put wisdom, that they may make all that I have commanded
thee: the tent of meeting, and the ark of the testimony, and 7
the mercy-seat that is thereupon, and all the furniture of the
Tent; and the table and its vessels, and the pure candle- 8
stick with all its vessels, and the altar of incense; and the 9
altar of burnt offering with all its vessels, and the laver and
its base; and the finely wrought garments, and the holy 10
garments for Aaron the priest, and the garments of his sons,
to minister in the priest's office; and the anointing oil, and 11
the incense of sweet spices for the holy place: according
to all that I have commanded thee shall they do.

12–17. *The keeping of the sabbath.*

And the LORD spake unto Moses, saying, Speak thou 12
also unto the children of Israel, saying, Verily ye shall keep 13
my sabbaths: for it is a sign between me and you throughout

---

xxxi. 2. Bezalel. The name = 'In the shadow (i.e. care) of God.'
Hur. Not to be identified with the Hur of xvii. 10, xxiv. 14.
3. I have filled him. See on xxviii. 3.
6. Oholiab. Gray thinks this name is of foreign origin (*Hebrew
Proper Names*, p. 246). It would seem to mean 'The Father
(i.e. God) is my tent.'
13. it is a sign. 'The sabbath, as a day observed weekly in
honour of Jehovah, and kept sacred to Him, is a constantly

your generations ; that ye may know that I am the LORD
14 which sanctify you. Ye shall keep the sabbath therefore;
for it is holy unto you: every one that profaneth it shall
surely be put to death : for whosoever doeth any work
therein, that soul shall be cut off from among his people.
15 Six days shall work be done; but on the seventh day is a
sabbath of solemn rest, holy to the LORD: whosoever
doeth any work in the sabbath day, he shall surely be put
16 to death. Wherefore the children of Israel shall keep the
sabbath, to observe the sabbath throughout their genera-
17 tions, for a perpetual covenant. It is a sign between me
and the children of Israel for ever: for in six days the
LORD made heaven and earth, and on the seventh day he
rested, and was refreshed.

18. *Moses receives the tables of the law.*

18   And he gave unto Moses, when he had made an end of
communing with him upon mount Sinai, the two tables of
the testimony, tables of stone, written with the finger of
God.

xxxii. 1–6. *The making of the golden calf.*

32   And when the people saw that Moses delayed to come
down from the mount, the people gathered themselves together unto Aaron, and said unto him, Up, make us gods,
which shall go before us; for as for this Moses, the man
that brought us up out of the land of Egypt, we know not
2 what is become of him. And Aaron said unto them, Break

---

recurring memorial of Israel's dedication to Him, and of the
covenant-relation subsisting between them' (Driver). See notes
on xx. 10 and the writer's *Jeremiah*, pp. 143 f.

xxxii. 1. gods. The Heb. for God is always in the plural;
here however it is used with a plural *verb*, hence the English
rendering.

Moses, the man. Cf. the similar but slightly different phrase
in xi. 3; Numb. xii. 3.

off the golden rings, which are in the ears of your wives, of
your sons, and of your daughters, and bring them unto me.
And all the people brake off the golden rings which were 3
in their ears, and brought them unto Aaron. And he 4
received it at their hand, and fashioned it with a graving
tool, and made it a molten calf: and they said, These be
thy gods, O Israel, which brought thee up out of the land
of Egypt. And when Aaron saw *this*, he built an altar 5
before it; and Aaron made proclamation, and said, To-
morrow shall be a feast to the LORD. And they rose up 6
early on the morrow, and offered burnt offerings, and
brought peace offerings ; and the people sat down to eat
and to drink, and rose up to play.

7–14. *Jehovah's indignation.*

And the LORD spake unto Moses, Go, get thee down ; 7
for thy people, which thou broughtest up out of the land
of Egypt, have corrupted themselves : they have turned 8
aside quickly out of the way which I commanded them :
they have made them a molten calf, and have worshipped
it, and have sacrificed unto it, and said, These be thy gods,
O Israel, which brought thee up out of the land of Egypt.
And the LORD said unto Moses, I have seen this people, 9
and, behold, it is a stiffnecked people : now therefore let 10
me alone, that my wrath may wax hot against them, and

---

2. golden rings. The Koran forbids the wearing of gold
ornaments. See Burton, *Pilgrimage to Al-madinah*, etc. I. p. 34.

4. graving tool. The same word is translated 'pen' in Isa. viii. 1.

calf. A better rendering would be 'young bull.' This figure was
quite clearly intended to represent Jehovah (see next *v.*) and His
worship under such a form survived in the Northern Kingdom to
the very end (cf. 1 Kings xii. 28 f.; 2 Kings x. 29, xvii. 16;
Hos. viii. 5 f., x. 5, xiii. 2). As the Israelites seem to have been
without cattle in the wilderness period the bull worship was probably borrowed later from the Canaanites.

5. the LORD: lit. 'Jehovah' as always: cf. iii. 2.

7. thy people. Jehovah repudiates Israel: cf. Numb. xi. 12.

that I may consume them: and I will make of thee a great
11 nation. And Moses besought the LORD his God, and said,
LORD, why doth thy wrath wax hot against thy people,
which thou hast brought forth out of the land of Egypt
12 with great power and with a mighty hand? Wherefore
should the Egyptians speak, saying, For evil did he bring
them forth, to slay them in the mountains, and to consume
them from the face of the earth? Turn from thy fierce wrath,
13 and repent of this evil against thy people. Remember
Abraham, Isaac, and Israel, thy servants, to whom thou
swarest by thine own self, and saidst unto them, I will
multiply your seed as the stars of heaven, and all this land
that I have spoken of will I give unto your seed, and they
14 shall inherit it for ever. And the LORD repented of the
evil which he said he would do unto his people.

15–35. *The punishment of the people.*

15   And Moses turned, and went down from the mount,
with the two tables of the testimony in his hand; tables
that were written on both their sides; on the one side and
16 on the other were they written. And the tables were the
work of God, and the writing was the writing of God,
17 graven upon the tables. And when Joshua heard the noise
of the people as they shouted, he said unto Moses, There
18 is a noise of war in the camp. And he said, It is not the
voice of them that shout for mastery, neither is it the voice
of them that cry for being overcome: but the noise of them
19 that sing do I hear. And it came to pass, as soon as he
came nigh unto the camp, that he saw the calf and the
dancing: and Moses' anger waxed hot, and he cast the

---

10. of thee. The same proposal in Numb. xiv. 12.

14. repented. So in Deut. xxxii. 36; 2 Sam. xxiv. 16; Amos
vii. 3, 6. Balaam, however, regarded Jehovah as unchanging in
purpose (Numb. xxiii. 19; cf. 1 Sam. xv. 29). The reconciliation
of this apparent contradiction is to be found in Jer. xxvi. 3.

19. dancing. See on xv. 21.

tables out of his hands, and brake them beneath the mount.
And he took the calf which they had made, and burnt it 20
with fire, and ground it to powder, and strewed it upon the
water, and made the children of Israel drink of it. And 21
Moses said unto Aaron, What did this people unto thee,
that thou hast brought a great sin upon them? And Aaron 22
said, Let not the anger of my lord wax hot: thou knowest
the people, that they are *set* on evil. For they said unto 23
me, Make us gods, which shall go before us: for as for
this Moses, the man that brought us up out of the land of
Egypt, we know not what is become of him. And I said 24
unto them, Whosoever hath any gold, let them break it
off; so they gave it me: and I cast it into the fire, and
there came out this calf. And when Moses saw that the 25
people were broken loose; for Aaron had let them loose
for a derision among their enemies: then Moses stood in 26
the gate of the camp, and said, Whoso is on the LORD's
side, *let him come* unto me. And all the sons of Levi
gathered themselves together unto him. And he said unto 27
them, Thus saith the LORD, the God of Israel, Put ye every
man his sword upon his thigh, and go to and fro from gate
to gate throughout the camp, and slay every man his
brother, and every man his companion, and every man his
neighbour. And the sons of Levi did according to the word 28
of Moses: and there fell of the people that day about three
thousand men. And Moses said, Consecrate yourselves 29

---

20. burnt it...ground it. Probably the image had a wooden
core plated with gold.

24. Aaron's excuses are very contemptible.

25. broken loose. Either by openly defying authority (cf.
Numb. xiv. 4) or by fighting amongst themselves.

derision. The marg. 'whispering' is expressive.

26. on the LORD's side. The circumstances of the narrative
are obscure; in the Calf incident there had been no repudiation
of Jehovah. Many scholars think *vv.* 25–29 are out of their
context.

28. the sons of Levi. Cf. the zeal of Phinehas (Numb. xxv. 7 ff.).

to-day to the LORD, yea, every man against his son, and against his brother; that he may bestow upon you a
30 blessing this day. And it came to pass on the morrow, that Moses said unto the people, Ye have sinned a great sin: and now I will go up unto the LORD; peradventure
31 I shall make atonement for your sin. And Moses returned unto the LORD, and said, Oh, this people have sinned a
32 great sin, and have made them gods of gold. Yet now, if thou wilt forgive their sin—; and if not, blot me, I pray
33 thee, out of thy book which thou hast written. And the LORD said unto Moses, Whosoever hath sinned against
34 me, him will I blot out of my book. And now go, lead the people unto *the place* of which I have spoken unto thee: behold, mine angel shall go before thee: nevertheless in
35 the day when I visit, I will visit their sin upon them. And the LORD smote the people, because they made the calf, which Aaron made.

xxxiii. 1-6. *Jehovah refuses to go up with the people.*

33   And the LORD spake unto Moses, Depart, go up hence, thou and the people which thou hast brought up out of the land of Egypt, unto the land of which I sware unto Abraham, to Isaac, and to Jacob, saying, Unto thy seed will I
2 give it: and I will send an angel before thee; and I will drive out the Canaanite, the Amorite, and the Hittite, and
3 the Perizzite, the Hivite, and the Jebusite: unto a land flowing with milk and honey: for I will not go up in the

---

32. **out of thy book.** That is, cross me off the register of the living, 'let me die': so in Numb. xi. 15 Moses asks God to kill him. For the figure cf. Dan. xii. 1; Luke x. 20; Phil. iv. 3. In the last two quotations the book is a register, not of the 'living' but of those who are to inherit eternal life.

34. **mine angel.** See on iii. 2.

xxxiii. 2. **Canaanite**, etc. See notes on iii. 8.

3. **a land flowing**. See on iii. 8.

I will not go. Jehovah would remain at Sinai.

midst of thee; for thou art a stiffnecked people: lest I
consume thee in the way. And when the people heard 4
these evil tidings, they mourned: and no man did put on
him his ornaments. And the LORD said unto Moses, Say 5
unto the children of Israel, Ye are a stiffnecked people:
if I go up into the midst of thee for one moment, I shall
consume thee: therefore now put off thy ornaments from
thee, that I may know what to do unto thee. And the 6
children of Israel stripped themselves of their ornaments
from mount Horeb onward.

7–11. *The tent of meeting.*

Now Moses used to take the tent and to pitch it with- 7
out the camp, afar off from the camp; and he called it,
The tent of meeting. And it came to pass, that every one
which sought the LORD went out unto the tent of meeting,
which was without the camp. And it came to pass, when 8
Moses went out unto the Tent, that all the people rose up,
and stood, every man at his tent door, and looked after
Moses, until he was gone into the Tent. And it came to 9
pass, when Moses entered into the Tent, the pillar of cloud
descended, and stood at the door of the Tent: and *the*
LORD spake with Moses. And all the people saw the 10
pillar of cloud stand at the door of the Tent: and all the
people rose up and worshipped, every man at his tent door.
And the LORD spake unto Moses face to face, as a man 11
speaketh unto his friend. And he turned again into the

---

6. Horeb. See on iii. *1.*

7. The tent. An early account of the tent of meeting before the
elaborate conceptions of P had transformed it into the better-
known tabernacle: cf. xxv.–xxxi. To suppose that this tent is
something additional to the tabernacle creates more difficulties than
it avoids, though as McNeile admits the editor himself must 'have
adopted some such explanation for the harmonizing of the two
accounts.'

without the camp. P's tabernacle was in the centre of the camp
(cf. Numb. i. 50–ii. 34).

camp: but his minister Joshua, the son of Nun, a young
man, departed not out of the Tent.

12–23. *Moses sees the glory of Jehovah.*

12 And Moses said unto the LORD, See, thou sayest unto
me, Bring up this people: and thou hast not let me know
whom thou wilt send with me. Yet thou hast said, I know
thee by name, and thou hast also found grace in my sight.
13 Now therefore, I pray thee, if I have found grace in thy
sight, shew me now thy ways, that I may know thee, to the
end that I may find grace in thy sight: and consider that
14 this nation is thy people. And he said, My presence shall
15 go *with thee*, and I will give thee rest. And he said unto
him, If thy presence go not *with me*, carry us not up hence.
16 For wherein now shall it be known that I have found grace
in thy sight, I and thy people? is it not in that thou goest
with us, so that we be separated, I and thy people, from
all the people that are upon the face of the earth?
17 And the LORD said unto Moses, I will do this thing also
that thou hast spoken: for thou hast found grace in my
18 sight, and I know thee by name. And he said, Shew me,
19 I pray thee, thy glory. And he said, I will make all my
goodness pass before thee, and will proclaim the name of
the LORD before thee; and I will be gracious to whom I
will be gracious, and will shew mercy on whom I will shew
20 mercy. And he said, Thou canst not see my face: for man
21 shall not see me and live. And the LORD said, Behold,

---

11. Joshua, the son of Nun. Here introduced as if hitherto
unknown (see on xvii. 9). He evidently stood towards Moses in
much the same relationship as Samuel to Eli (1 Sam. iii. 1).
12. whom thou wilt send. Cf. however *v.* 2 and xxxii. 34.
14. presence. Lit. 'face,' i.e. Jehovah Himself (LXX αὐτός).
18. glory. The majesty of Jehovah.
19. goodness. Better 'beauty' or 'comeliness.'
name. In O.T. name often=character: cf. xxxiv. 14.
be gracious...shew mercy. See on xxxiv. 6.

there is a place by me, and thou shalt stand upon the rock :
and it shall come to pass, while my glory passeth by, that 22
I will put thee in a cleft of the rock, and will cover thee
with my hand until I have passed by : and I will take 23
away mine hand, and thou shalt see my back : but my
face shall not be seen.

xxxiv. 1-28. *The renewal of the covenant.*

And the LORD said unto Moses, Hew thee two tables **34**
of stone like unto the first : and I will write upon the tables
the words that were on the first tables, which thou brakest.
And be ready by the morning, and come up in the morning 2
unto mount Sinai, and present thyself there to me on the
top of the mount. And no man shall come up with thee, 3
neither let any man be seen throughout all the mount;
neither let the flocks nor herds feed before that mount.
And he hewed two tables of stone like unto the first; and 4
Moses rose up early in the morning, and went up unto
mount Sinai, as the LORD had commanded him, and took
in his hand two tables of stone. And the LORD descended 5
in the cloud, and stood with him there, and proclaimed the
name of the LORD. And the LORD passed by before him, 6
and proclaimed, The LORD, the LORD, a God full of compassion and gracious, slow to anger, and plenteous in mercy
and truth ; keeping mercy for thousands, forgiving iniquity 7
and transgression and sin : and that will by no means
clear *the guilty*; visiting the iniquity of the fathers upon

---

21. the rock. Cf. xvii. 6 where Jehovah promises to stand
before Moses.

xxxiv. 1. Hew thee. Jehovah Himself provided the former
tables of stone : xxxii. 16.

3. Cf. xix. 12 f.

6. The LORD, etc. One of the greatest passages in O.T. and
one which is constantly referred to or quoted: Numb. xiv. 18;
Jer. xxxii. 18; Joel ii. 31; Nah. i. 3, etc. and frequently in the
Psalms.

the children, and upon the children's children, upon the
8 third and upon the fourth generation. And Moses made
haste, and bowed his head toward the earth, and worshipped.
9 And he said, If now I have found grace in thy sight, O
Lord, let the Lord, I pray thee, go in the midst of us; for
it is a stiffnecked people; and pardon our iniquity and our
10 sin, and take us for thine inheritance. And he said, Behold,
I make a covenant: before all thy people I will do marvels,
such as have not been wrought in all the earth, nor in any
nation: and all the people among which thou art shall see
the work of the LORD, for it is a terrible thing that I do
11 with thee. Observe thou that which I command thee this
day: behold, I drive out before thee the Amorite, and the
Canaanite, and the Hittite, and the Perizzite, and the Hivite,
12 and the Jebusite. Take heed to thyself, lest thou make a
covenant with the inhabitants of the land whither thou
13 goest, lest it be for a snare in the midst of thee: but ye
shall break down their altars, and dash in pieces their
14 pillars, and ye shall cut down their Asherim: for thou shalt
worship no other god: for the LORD, whose name is Jealous,
15 is a jealous God: lest thou make a covenant with the inhabitants of the land, and they go a whoring after their
gods, and do sacrifice unto their gods, and one call thee
16 and thou eat of his sacrifice; and thou take of their daughters unto thy sons, and their daughters go a whoring after
their gods, and make thy sons go a whoring after their gods.
17,18 Thou shalt make thee no molten gods. The feast of unleavened bread shalt thou keep. Seven days thou shalt
eat unleavened bread, as I commanded thee, at the time
appointed in the month Abib: for in the month Abib thou
19 camest out from Egypt. All that openeth the womb is

---

13. Asherim. Wooden posts set up beside Canaanite altars,
possibly to represent sacred trees.
14. a jealous God. See on xx. 5.
18. unleavened bread. See on xxiii. 14 ff.

mine; and all thy cattle that is male, the firstlings of ox
and sheep. And the firstling of an ass thou shalt redeem 20
with a lamb : and if thou wilt not redeem it, then thou shalt
break its neck. All the firstborn of thy sons thou shalt
redeem. And none shall appear before me empty. Six days 21
thou shalt work, but on the seventh day thou shalt rest : in
plowing time and in harvest thou shalt rest. And thou shalt 22
observe the feast of weeks, *even* of the firstfruits of wheat
harvest, and the feast of ingathering at the year's end.
Three times in the year shall all thy males appear before 23
the Lord GOD, the God of Israel. For I will cast out nations 24
before thee, and enlarge thy borders : neither shall any man
desire thy land, when thou goest up to appear before the
LORD thy God three times in the year. Thou shalt not 25
offer the blood of my sacrifice with leavened bread ; neither
shall the sacrifice of the feast of the passover be left unto
the morning. The first of the firstfruits of thy ground thou 26
shalt bring unto the house of the LORD thy God. Thou
shalt not seethe a kid in its mother's milk. And the LORD 27
said unto Moses, Write thou these words : for after the
tenor of these words I have made a covenant with thee and
with Israel. And he was there with the LORD forty days 28
and forty nights ; he did neither eat bread, nor drink water.
And he wrote upon the tables the words of the covenant,
the ten commandments.

---

19. firstlings. See on xiii. 13, xxii. 29 f.
22. feast of weeks. Called feast of harvest in xxiii. 16.
24. when thou goest up. This suggests a long journey and
must belong to the days when the local sanctuaries had been
abolished by the Deuteronomic reformation and all worship con-
centrated at Jerusalem.
26. See on xxiii. 19.
27. Write thou. Cf. *v.* 1.
28. the ten commandments. This must refer to the commands contained in *vv.* 11 ff. if the text is to be followed,
probably however the words are a later addition.

29-35. The shining of Moses' face.

29 And it came to pass, when Moses came down from mount
Sinai with the two tables of the testimony in Moses' hand,
when he came down from the mount, that Moses wist not
that the skin of his face shone by reason of his speaking
30 with him. And when Aaron and all the children of Israel
saw Moses, behold, the skin of his face shone; and they
31 were afraid to come nigh him. And Moses called unto
them; and Aaron and all the rulers of the congregation
32 returned unto him: and Moses spake to them. And after-
ward all the children of Israel came nigh: and he gave them
in commandment all that the LORD had spoken with him
33 in mount Sinai. And when Moses had done speaking with
34 them, he put a veil on his face. But when Moses went in
before the LORD to speak with him, he took the veil off,
until he came out; and he came out, and spake unto the
35 children of Israel that which he was commanded; and the
children of Israel saw the face of Moses, that the skin of
Moses' face shone: and Moses put the veil upon his face
again, until he went in to speak with him.

xxxv. 1-3. The sabbath to be observed.

35 And Moses assembled all the congregation of the children of Israel, and said unto them, These are the words

---

29. shone: lit. 'sent forth horns' (=rays: cf. Hab. iii. 4).
Vulg. translated lit. *cornuta*. McNeile cites Michael Angelo's
famous statue of Moses with horns in San Pietro in Vincoli at
Rome, a representation due to the Vulgate rendering.

33. put a veil. In order that the Israelites might not see the
glow. St Paul interprets differently (2 Cor. iii. 7 ff.) and makes
the function of the veil that of concealing the dying away of the
glow.

xxxv.-xl. These chapters contain an account of the carrying
out of the commands in xxv.-xxxi. There are some changes of
order and some slight verbal alterations. The LXX and the
Heb. of these chapters contain striking differences: see the table
in McNeile, pp. 224 f.

which the LORD hath commanded, that ye should do them.
Six days shall work be done, but on the seventh day there 2
shall be to you an holy day, a sabbath of solemn rest to
the LORD : whosoever doeth any work therein shall be put
to death. Ye shall kindle no fire throughout your habitations 3
upon the sabbath day.

4–29. *Appeal for offerings and labour.*

And Moses spake unto all the congregation of the chil- 4
dren of Israel, saying, This is the thing which the LORD
commanded, saying, Take ye from among you an offering 5
unto the LORD : whosoever is of a willing heart, let him
bring it, the LORD'S offering ; gold, and silver, and brass ;
and blue, and purple, and scarlet, and fine linen, and goats' 6
hair ; and rams' skins dyed red, and sealskins, and acacia 7
wood ; and oil for the light, and spices for the anointing 8
oil, and for the sweet incense ; and onyx stones, and stones 9
to be set, for the ephod, and for the breastplate. And let 10
every wise hearted man among you come, and make all
that the LORD hath commanded ; the tabernacle, its tent, 11
and its covering, its clasps, and its boards, its bars, its pillars, and its sockets ; the ark, and the staves thereof, the 12
mercy-seat, and the veil of the screen ; the table, and its 13
staves, and all its vessels, and the shewbread ; the candle- 14
stick also for the light, and its vessels, and its lamps, and
the oil for the light ; and the altar of incense, and its staves, 15
and the anointing oil, and the sweet incense, and the screen
for the door, at the door of the tabernacle ; the altar of 16
burnt offering, with its grating of brass, its staves, and all
its vessels, the laver and its base ; the hangings of the 17
court, the pillars thereof, and their sockets, and the screen

---

xxxv. 3. no fire. An interpretation of xvi. 23.

12. of the screen. These words are added.

15. the altar of incense. Notice that this has been moved
into a more fitting place in the narrative : cf. xxx. 1.

B E   9

18 for the gate of the court; the pins of the tabernacle, and
19 the pins of the court, and their cords; the finely wrought
garments, for ministering in the holy place, the holy garments for Aaron the priest, and the garments of his sons,
to minister in the priest's office.

20   And all the congregation of the children of Israel de-
21 parted from the presence of Moses. And they came, every
one whose heart stirred him up, and every one whom his
spirit made willing, *and* brought the LORD'S offering, for
the work of the tent of meeting, and for all the service
22 thereof, and for the holy garments. And they came, both
men and women, as many as were willing hearted, *and*
brought brooches, and earrings, and signet-rings, and
armlets, all jewels of gold; even every man that offered
23 an offering of gold unto the LORD. And every man, with
whom was found blue, and purple, and scarlet, and fine
linen, and goats' *hair*, and rams' skins dyed red, and seal-
24 skins, brought them. Every one that did offer an offering
of silver and brass brought the LORD'S offering: and every
man, with whom was found acacia wood for any work of
25 the service, brought it. And all the women that were wise
hearted did spin with their hands, and brought that which
they had spun, the blue, and the purple, the scarlet, and
26 the fine linen. And all the women whose heart stirred them
27 up in wisdom spun the goats' *hair*. And the rulers brought
the onyx stones, and the stones to be set, for the ephod,
28 and for the breastplate; and the spice, and the oil; for the
light, and for the anointing oil, and for the sweet incense.
29 The children of Israel brought a freewill offering unto the
LORD; every man and woman, whose heart made them
willing to bring for all the work, which the LORD had
commanded to be made by the hand of Moses.

---

18. **cords.** Not previously mentioned.

xxxv. 30–xxxvi. 7. *The appointment of the workmen.*

And Moses said unto the children of Israel, See, the 30
LORD hath called by name Bezalel the son of Uri, the
son of Hur, of the tribe of Judah; and he hath filled him 31
with the spirit of God, in wisdom, in understanding, and
in knowledge, and in all manner of workmanship; and to 32
devise cunning works, to work in gold, and in silver, and
in brass, and in cutting of stones for setting, and in carv- 33
ing of wood, to work in all manner of cunning workmanship.
And he hath put in his heart that he may teach, both he, 34
and Oholiab, the son of Ahisamach, of the tribe of Dan.
Them hath he filled with wisdom of heart, to work all 35
manner of workmanship, of the engraver, and of the
cunning workman, and of the embroiderer, in blue, and in
purple, in scarlet, and in fine linen, and of the weaver,
even of them that do any workmanship, and of those that
devise cunning works. And Bezalel and Oholiab shall **36**
work, and every wise hearted man, in whom the LORD
hath put wisdom and understanding to know how to work
all the work for the service of the sanctuary, according to
all that the LORD hath commanded.

And Moses called Bezalel and Oholiab, and every wise 2
hearted man, in whose heart the LORD had put wisdom,
even every one whose heart stirred him up to come unto
the work to do it: and they received of Moses all the 3
offering, which the children of Israel had brought for the
work of the service of the sanctuary, to make it withal.
And they brought yet unto him freewill offerings every
morning. And all the wise men, that wrought all the work 4
of the sanctuary, came every man from his work which
they wrought; and they spake unto Moses, saying, The 5
people bring much more than enough for the service of
the work, which the LORD commanded to make. And 6

---

34. that he may teach. Not stated elsewhere.

Moses gave commandment, and they caused it to be proclaimed throughout the camp, saying, Let neither man
nor woman make any more work for the offering of the
sanctuary. So the people were restrained from bringing.
7 For the stuff they had was sufficient for all the work to
make it, and too much.

xxxvi. 8–38. *The making of the tabernacle.*

8   And every wise hearted man among them that wrought
the work made the tabernacle with ten curtains; of fine
twined linen, and blue, and purple, and scarlet, with
cherubim the work of the cunning workman made he
9 them. The length of each curtain was eight and twenty
cubits, and the breadth of each curtain four cubits: all the
10 curtains had one measure. And he coupled five curtains
one to another: and *the other* five curtains he coupled one
11 to another. And he made loops of blue upon the edge of
the one curtain from the selvedge in the coupling: likewise he made in the edge of the curtain that was outmost
12 in the second coupling. Fifty loops made he in the one
curtain, and fifty loops made he in the edge of the curtain
that was in the second coupling: the loops were opposite
13 one to another. And he made fifty clasps of gold, and
coupled the curtains one to another with the clasps: so the
14 tabernacle was one. And he made curtains of goats' *hair*
for a tent over the tabernacle: eleven curtains he made
15 them. The length of each curtain was thirty cubits, and
four cubits the breadth of each curtain: the eleven curtains
16 had one measure. And he coupled five curtains by them-
17 selves, and six curtains by themselves. And he made fifty
loops on the edge of the curtain that was outmost in the
coupling, and fifty loops made he upon the edge of the
18 curtain which was *outmost in* the second coupling. And
he made fifty clasps of brass to couple the tent together,
19 that it might be one. And he made a covering for the tent

of rams' skins dyed red, and a covering of sealskins
above.

And he made the boards for the tabernacle of acacia 20
wood, standing up. Ten cubits was the length of a board, 21
and a cubit and a half the breadth of each board. Each 22
board had two tenons, joined one to another: thus did he
make for all the boards of the tabernacle. And he made 23
the boards for the tabernacle; twenty boards for the south
side southward: and he made forty sockets of silver under 24
the twenty boards; two sockets under one board for its
two tenons, and two sockets under another board for its
two tenons. And for the second side of the tabernacle, on 25
the north side, he made twenty boards, and their forty 26
sockets of silver; two sockets under one board, and two
sockets under another board. And for the hinder part of 27
the tabernacle westward he made six boards. And two 28
boards made he for the corners of the tabernacle in the
hinder part. And they were double beneath, and in like 29
manner they were entire unto the top thereof unto one
ring: thus he did to both of them in the two corners.
And there were eight boards, and their sockets of silver, 30
sixteen sockets; under every board two sockets. And he 31
made bars of acacia wood; five for the boards of the one
side of the tabernacle, and five bars for the boards of the 32
other side of the tabernacle, and five bars for the boards
of the tabernacle for the hinder part westward. And he 33
made the middle bar to pass through in the midst of the
boards from the one end to the other. And he overlaid 34
the boards with gold, and made their rings of gold for
places for the bars, and overlaid the bars with gold.

And he made the veil of blue, and purple, and scarlet, 35
and fine twined linen: with cherubim the work of the cunning workman made he it. And he made thereunto four 36
pillars of acacia, and overlaid them with gold: their hooks
were of gold; and he cast for them four sockets of silver.

37 And he made a screen for the door of the Tent, of blue,
and purple, and scarlet, and fine twined linen, the work of
38 the embroiderer; and the five pillars of it with their hooks:
and he overlaid their chapiters and their fillets with gold:
and their five sockets were of brass.

xxxvii. 1–29. *The ark and other furniture.*

27 And Bezalel made the ark of acacia wood: two cubits
and a half was the length of it, and a cubit and a half the
2 breadth of it, and a cubit and a half the height of it: and
he overlaid it with pure gold within and without, and made
3 a crown of gold to it round about. And he cast for it four
rings of gold, in the four feet thereof; even two rings on
the one side of it, and two rings on the other side of it.
4 And he made staves of acacia wood, and overlaid them
5 with gold. And he put the staves into the rings on the sides
6 of the ark, to bear the ark. And he made a mercy-seat of
pure gold: two cubits and a half *was* the length thereof,
7 and a cubit and a half the breadth thereof. And he made
two cherubim of gold; of beaten work made he them, at
8 the two ends of the mercy-seat; one cherub at the one
end, and one cherub at the other end: of one piece with
the mercy-seat made he the cherubim at the two ends
9 thereof. And the cherubim spread out their wings on high,
covering the mercy-seat with their wings, with their faces
one to another; toward the mercy-seat were the faces of
the cherubim.
10 And he made the table of acacia wood: two cubits *was*
the length thereof, and a cubit the breadth thereof, and a
11 cubit and a half the height thereof: and he overlaid it with
pure gold, and made thereto a crown of gold round about.
12 And he made unto it a border of an handbreadth round

---

xxxvii. 1. Bezalel made the ark. In Deut. x. 3 Moses himself
makes the ark *before* going up the mount; here Bezalel makes it
after the descent of Moses: see further, Driver, *Deut.* pp. 177 f.

about, and made a golden crown to the border thereof
round about. And he cast for it four rings of gold, and put 13
the rings in the four corners that were on the four feet thereof. Close by the border were the rings, the places for the 14
staves to bear the table. And he made the staves of acacia 15
wood, and overlaid them with gold, to bear the table. And 16
he made the vessels which were upon the table, the dishes
thereof, and the spoons thereof, and the bowls thereof, and
the flagons thereof, to pour out withal, of pure gold.

And he made the candlestick of pure gold: of beaten 17
work made he the candlestick, even its base, and its shaft ;
its cups, its knops, and its flowers, were of one piece with
it: and there were six branches going out of the sides 18
thereof ; three branches of the candlestick out of the one
side thereof, and three branches of the candlestick out of
the other side thereof: three cups made like almond- 19
blossoms in one branch, a knop and a flower ; and three
cups made like almond-blossoms in the other branch, a
knop and a flower: so for the six branches going out of
the candlestick. And in the candlestick were four cups 20
made like almond-blossoms, the knops thereof, and the
flowers thereof: and a knop under two branches of one 21
piece with it, and a knop under two branches of one piece
with it, and a knop under two branches of one piece with
it, for the six branches going out of it. Their knops and 22
their branches were of one piece with it: the whole of it
was one beaten work of pure gold. And he made the 23
lamps thereof, seven, and the tongs thereof, and the snuffdishes thereof, of pure gold. Of a talent of pure gold made 24
he it, and all the vessels thereof.

And he made the altar of incense of acacia wood: a 25
cubit was the length thereof, and a cubit the breadth thereof, foursquare ; and two cubits was the height thereof; the
horns thereof were of one piece with it. And he overlaid 26
it with pure gold, the top thereof, and the sides thereof

round about, and the horns of it : and he made unto it a

27 crown of gold round about. And he made for it two golden rings under the crown thereof, upon the two ribs thereof, upon the two sides of it, for places for staves to bear it

28 withal. And he made the staves of acacia wood, and over-

29 laid them with gold. And he made the holy anointing oil, and the pure incense of sweet spices, after the art of the perfumer.

xxxviii. 1–8. *The altar of burnt offering and the bronze laver.*

38 And he made the altar of burnt offering of acacia wood : five cubits was the length thereof, and five cubits the breadth thereof, foursquare; and three cubits the height

2 thereof. And he made the horns thereof upon the four corners of it; the horns thereof were of one piece with it:

3 and he overlaid it with brass. And he made all the vessels of the altar, the pots, and the shovels, and the basons, the fleshhooks, and the firepans : all the vessels thereof made

4 he of brass. And he made for the altar a grating of net-work of brass, under the ledge round it beneath, reaching

5 halfway up. And he cast four rings for the four ends of

6 the grating of brass, to be places for the staves. And he made the staves of acacia wood, and overlaid them with

7 brass. And he put the staves into the rings on the sides of the altar, to bear it withal; he made it hollow with planks.

8 And he made the laver of brass, and the base thereof of brass, of the mirrors of the serving women which served at the door of the tent of meeting.

---

xxxviii. 2. overlaid it with brass. In Numb. xvi. 36 ff. the covering is made from the censers of Korah and his company. LXX inserts a statement more to that effect, forgetting that Korah's rebellion took place much later.

8. which served. Lit. 'which *warred*.' Used of Levites in Numb. iv. 1 ff. etc.

9–20. *The court.*

And he made the court: for the south side southward 9
the hangings of the court were of fine twined linen, an
hundred cubits: their pillars were twenty, and their sockets 10
twenty, of brass; the hooks of the pillars and their fillets
were of silver. And for the north side an hundred cubits, 11
their pillars twenty, and their sockets twenty, of brass;
the hooks of the pillars and their fillets of silver. And for 12
the west side were hangings of fifty cubits, their pillars
ten, and their sockets ten; the hooks of the pillars and
their fillets of silver. And for the east side eastward fifty 13
cubits. The hangings for the one side *of the gate* were 14
fifteen cubits; their pillars three, and their sockets three;
and o for the other side: on this hand and that hand by 15
the gate of the court were hangings of fifteen cubits; their
pillars three, and their sockets three. All the hangings of 16
the court round about were of fine twined linen. And the 17
sockets for the pillars were of brass; the hooks of the
pillars and their fillets of silver; and the overlaying of their
chapiters of silver; and all the pillars of the court were
filleted with silver. And the screen for the gate of the 18
court was the work of the embroiderer, of blue, and purple,
and scarlet, and fine twined linen: and twenty cubits was
the length, and the height in the breadth was five cubits,
answerable to the hangings of the court. And their pillars 19
were four, and their sockets four, of brass; their hooks of
silver, and the overlaying of their chapiters and their fillets
of silver. And all the pins of the tabernacle, and of the 20
court round about, were of brass.

21–31. *The metal used for the work.*

This is the sum of *the things for* the tabernacle, even 21
the tabernacle of the testimony, as they were counted, according to the commandment of Moses, for the service of

the Levites, by the hand of Ithamar, the son of Aaron the
22 priest. And Bezalel the son of Uri, the son of Hur, of the
tribe of Judah, made all that the LORD commanded Moses.
23 And with him was Oholiab, the son of Ahisamach, of the
tribe of Dan, an engraver, and a cunning workman, and
an embroiderer in blue, and in purple, and in scarlet, and
fine linen.
24   All the gold that was used for the work in all the work
of the sanctuary, even the gold of the offering, was twenty
and nine talents, and seven hundred and thirty shekels,
25 after the shekel of the sanctuary. And the silver of them
that were numbered of the congregation was an hundred
talents, and a thousand seven hundred and threescore and
26 fifteen shekels, after the shekel of the sanctuary : a beka
a head, *that is*, half a shekel, after the shekel of the sanctuary, for every one that passed over to them that were
numbered, from twenty years old and upward, for six
hundred thousand and three thousand and five hundred
27 and fifty men. And the hundred talents of silver were for
casting the sockets of the sanctuary, and the sockets of
the veil ; an hundred sockets for the hundred talents, a
28 talent for a socket. And of the thousand seven hundred
seventy and five *shekels* he made hooks for the pillars, and
29 overlaid their chapiters, and made fillets for them. And
the brass of the offering was seventy talents, and two
30 thousand and four hundred shekels. And therewith he
made the sockets to the door of the tent of meeting, and
the brasen altar, and the brasen grating for it, and all
31 the vessels of the altar, and the sockets of the court round
about, and the sockets of the gate of the court, and all the
pins of the tabernacle, and all the pins of the court round
about.

---

21. the Levites. Elsewhere in this book iv. 14, xxxii. 25 ff.
only : Numb. i. 49 f. is presupposed.
26. that were numbered. This presupposes Numb. i. 46 ff.

xxxix. 1–31. *The priestly vestments.*

And of the blue, and purple, and scarlet, they made **39**
finely wrought garments, for ministering in the holy place,
and made the holy garments for Aaron; as the LORD
commanded Moses.

And he made the ephod of gold, blue, and purple, and 2
scarlet, and fine twined linen. And they did beat the gold 3
into thin plates, and cut it into wires, to work it in the blue,
and in the purple, and in the scarlet, and in the fine linen,
the work of the cunning workman. They made shoulder- 4
pieces for it, joined together: at the two ends was it joined
together. And the cunningly woven band, that was upon 5
it, to gird it on withal, was of the same piece *and* like the
work thereof; of gold, of blue, and purple, and scarlet, and
fine twined linen; as the LORD commanded Moses.

And they wrought the onyx stones, inclosed in ouches 6
of gold, graven with the engravings of a signet, according
to the names of the children of Israel. And he put them 7
on the shoulderpieces of the ephod, to be stones of memorial
for the children of Israel; as the LORD commanded
Moses.

And he made the breastplate, the work of the cunning 8
workman, like the work of the ephod; of gold, of blue, and
purple, and scarlet, and fine twined linen. It was four- 9
square; they made the breastplate double: a span was
the length thereof, and a span the breadth thereof, being
double. And they set in it four rows of stones: a row of 10
sardius, topaz, and carbuncle was the first row. And the 11
second row, an emerald, a sapphire, and a diamond. And 12
the third row, a jacinth, an agate, and an amethyst. And 13
the fourth row, a beryl, an onyx, and a jasper: they were
inclosed in ouches of gold in their settings. And the stones 14
were according to the names of the children of Israel,
welve, according to their names; like the engravings of

a signet, every one according to his name, for the twelve
15 tribes. And they made upon the breastplate chains like
16 cords, of wreathen work of pure gold. And they made two
ouches of gold, and two gold rings; and put the two rings
17 on the two ends of the breastplate. And they put the two
wreathen chains of gold on the two rings at the ends of
18 the breastplate. And the *other* two ends of the two
wreathen chains they put on the two ouches, and put them
on the shoulderpieces of the ephod, in the forepart thereof.
19 And they made two rings of gold, and put them upon the
two ends of the breastplate, upon the edge thereof, which
20 was toward the side of the ephod inward. And they made
two rings of gold, and put them on the two shoulderpieces
of the ephod underneath, in the forepart thereof, close by
the coupling thereof, above the cunningly woven band of
21 the ephod. And they did bind the breastplate by the rings
thereof unto the rings of the ephod with a lace of blue,
that it might be upon the cunningly woven band of the
ephod, and that the breastplate might not be loosed from
the ephod; as the LORD commanded Moses.

22   And he made the robe of the ephod of woven work, all
23 of blue; and the hole of the robe in the midst thereof, as
the hole of a coat of mail, with a binding round about the
24 hole of it, that it should not be rent. And they made upon
the skirts of the robe pomegranates of blue, and purple,
25 and scarlet, *and* twined *linen*. And they made bells of pure
gold, and put the bells between the pomegranates upon
the skirts of the robe round about, between the pome-
26 granates; a bell and a pomegranate, a bell and a pomegranate, upon the skirts of the robe round about, to minister
in; as the LORD commanded Moses.

27   And they made the coats of fine linen of woven work
28 for Aaron, and for his sons, and the mitre of fine linen, and
the goodly headtires of fine linen, and the linen breeches
29 of fine twined linen, and the girdle of fine twined linen,

and blue, and purple, and scarlet, the work of the embroiderer; as the LORD commanded Moses.

And they made the plate of the holy crown of pure gold, 30
and wrote upon it a writing, like the engravings of a signet,
HOLY TO THE LORD. And they tied unto it a lace of blue, 31
to fasten it upon the mitre above; as the LORD commanded
Moses.

32–43. *The finished work is brought to Moses.*

Thus was finished all the work of the tabernacle of the 32
tent of meeting: and the children of Israel did according
to all that the LORD commanded Moses, so did they.

And they brought the tabernacle unto Moses, the Tent, 33
and all its furniture, its clasps, its boards, its bars, and its
pillars, and its sockets; and the covering of rams' skins 34
dyed red, and the covering of sealskins, and the veil of
the screen; the ark of the testimony, and the staves there- 35
of, and the mercy-seat; the table, all the vessels thereof, 36
and the shewbread; the pure candlestick, the lamps 37
thereof, even the lamps to be set in order, and all the
vessels thereof, and the oil for the light; and the golden 38
altar, and the anointing oil, and the sweet incense, and
the screen for the door of the Tent; the brasen altar, and 39
its grating of brass, its staves, and all its vessels, the laver
and its base; the hangings of the court, its pillars, and its 40
sockets, and the screen for the gate of the court, the cords
thereof, and the pins thereof, and all the instruments of
the service of the tabernacle, for the tent of meeting; the 41
finely wrought garments for ministering in the holy place,
and the holy garments for Aaron the priest, and the garments of his sons, to minister in the priest's office. Ac- 42
cording to all that the LORD commanded Moses, so the
children of Israel did all the work. And Moses saw all the 43
work, and, behold, they had done it; as the LORD had

commanded, even so had they done it: and Moses blessed
them.

xl. 1-33.   *The setting up of the tabernacle.*

40 2   And the LORD spake unto Moses, saying, On the first
day of the first month shalt thou rear up the tabernacle of
3 the tent of meeting. And thou shalt put therein the ark of
the testimony, and thou shalt screen the ark with the veil.
4 And thou shalt bring in the table, and set in order the
things that are upon it; and thou shalt bring in the candle-
5 stick, and light the lamps thereof. And thou shalt set the
golden altar for incense before the ark of the testimony,
6 and put the screen of the door to the tabernacle. And thou
shalt set the altar of burnt offering before the door of the
7 tabernacle of the tent of meeting. And thou shalt set the
laver between the tent of meeting and the altar, and shalt
8 put water therein. And thou shalt set up the court round
about, and hang up the screen of the gate of the court.
9 And thou shalt take the anointing oil, and anoint the
tabernacle, and all that is therein, and shalt hallow it, and
10 all the furniture thereof: and it shall be holy. And thou
shalt anoint the altar of burnt offering, and all its vessels,
and sanctify the altar: and the altar shall be most holy.
11 And thou shalt anoint the laver and its base, and sanctify
12 it. And thou shalt bring Aaron and his sons unto the door
of the tent of meeting, and shalt wash them with water.
13 And thou shalt put upon Aaron the holy garments; and
thou shalt anoint him, and sanctify him, that he may
14 minister unto me in the priest's office. And thou shalt
15 bring his sons, and put coats upon them: and thou shalt
anoint them, as thou didst anoint their father, that they
may minister unto me in the priest's office: and their
anointing shall be to them for an everlasting priesthood

---

xl. 15. **anoint them.** See on xxix. 7.

throughout their generations. Thus did Moses: according 16
to all that the LORD commanded him, so did he.

And it came to pass in the first month in the second 17
year, on the first day of the month, that the tabernacle was
reared up. And Moses reared up the tabernacle, and laid 18
its sockets, and set up the boards thereof, and put in the
bars thereof, and reared up its pillars. And he spread the 19
tent over the tabernacle, and put the covering of the tent
above upon it; as the LORD commanded Moses. And he 20
took and put the testimony into the ark, and set the staves
on the ark, and put the mercy-seat above upon the ark:
and he brought the ark into the tabernacle, and set up the 21
veil of the screen, and screened the ark of the testimony;
as the LORD commanded Moses. And he put the table in 22
the tent of meeting, upon the side of the tabernacle north-
ward, without the veil. And he set the bread in order upon 23
it before the LORD; as the LORD commanded Moses. And 24
he put the candlestick in the tent of meeting, over against
the table, on the side of the tabernacle southward. And 25
he lighted the lamps before the LORD; as the LORD commanded Moses. And he put the golden altar in the tent 26
of meeting before the veil: and he burnt thereon incense 27
of sweet spices; as the LORD commanded Moses. And he 28
put the screen of the door to the tabernacle. And he set 29
the altar of burnt offering at the door of the tabernacle of
the tent of meeting, and offered upon it the burnt offering
and the meal offering; as the LORD commanded Moses.
And he set the laver between the tent of meeting and the 30
altar, and put water therein, to wash withal. And Moses 31
and Aaron and his sons washed their hands and their feet
thereat; when they went into the tent of meeting, and 32
when they came near unto the altar, they washed: as the
LORD commanded Moses. And he reared up the court 33

---

20. into the ark. Cf. Deut. x. 3.

round about the tabernacle and the altar, and set up the
screen of the gate of the court. So Moses finished the
work.

34–38. *The cloud descends upon the tabernacle.*

34 Then the cloud covered the tent of meeting, and the
35 glory of the LORD filled the tabernacle. And Moses was
not able to enter into the tent of meeting, because the
cloud abode thereon, and the glory of the LORD filled the
36 tabernacle. And when the cloud was taken up from over
the tabernacle, the children of Israel went onward, through-
37 out all their journeys: but if the cloud were not taken up,
then they journeyed not till the day that it was taken up.
38 For the cloud of the LORD was upon the tabernacle by
day, and there was fire therein by night, in the sight of all
the house of Israel, throughout all their journeys.

---

36 f. Cf. Numb. x. 34.

38. The dwelling and all its furniture being finished Jehovah
takes up His abode in the midst of His people—a fitting climax
to the book of Exodus.

INDEX

Aaron 95, 102, 121
Abib, the month, 50, 56
Abihu 36, 90
altar of incense 113, 129
altars 79 f., 100 f.
Amalek 70
Amorites 26
angel of God 60
angel of the LORD 25
anointing oil 115
anthropomorphisms 9, 61
Aperu 6 f.
ark 69, 94
Asherim 126
atonement 111

Baal-zephon 58
Baentsch 75, 81, 109
bells of gold 106
beryl 105
between the two evenings 3, 50
Bezalel 117, 134
bitter herbs 51
bitumen 22
blue 93
boils 43
Book of the Covenant 10, 91
brass 93
breastplate 93, 104
brickmaking 32
burnt offerings 79
bush, burning, 25

calamus 115
camels 43
Canaanites 12, 26
candlestick, the golden, 96
carbuncle 104

cassia 115
census 114
cherubim 92
circumcision 31
cloud 58
coat of high-priest 107
consecrate 107
coriander seed 68
covenant 75
Covenant, Book of the, 10, 91
cubit 94

daily offering 112
dances 64, 120
Decalogue, the 77 f., 127
Deuteronomic expressions in Exodus 4
devote 85
diamond 105
diseases of Egypt 65
dowry 85
Driver 5, etc.
dukes of Edom 63

E 4 f.
Egypt, contemporary history of, 15 f.
elders 27
Eleazar 103
Elim 65
emerald 105
ephod 93, 103
Etham 58
Exodus, book of:
    name 1
    sources 1 ff., 18
    contents 17 f.
    historical value 5 ff.
    religious value 8 ff.

Exodus, the 6 f.
Ezekiel 9, 112

fallow year 12, 88
feast (=pilgrimage) 32
feasts:
    unleavened bread 88
    harvest 88
    ingathering 88
fill the hands (=consecrate) 107
fillets 101
fire, a symbol of the divine presence 25, 76
firstborn, sacrifice of, 86
firstfruits 86
firstlings 87
flax 45
flies in Egypt 41
Flinders Petrie 20, 54, 106
flint knife 31
forty days 92
Frazer, J. G. 22, 24, 36, 81, 89, 106, 114
frogs 39
frontlets 57

galbanum 116
Gershom 24
glory of the LORD 92
God Almighty (*El Shaddai*) 34
golden calf 118 f.
Goshen 41

H 3
Hammurabi, code of 84
Hamsīn 48
hands laid on sacrifice 108
heave-offering 110
hin 112
Hittites 15, 26
Hivites 26, 90
holiness 87, 111
honey 26
Horeb 25, 70
hornet, the, 90

horns of altar 100
Hur 70
Hur, grandfather of Bezalel 117
Hyksos 15
hyssop 52

incense 113
Israelites in Egypt:
    length of sojourn 6 f.
    numbers 7, 54, 73
Ithamar 103

J 4 f.
jacinth 105
Jannes and Jambres 37
JE 4
jealousy, of God, 77
Jebel Mūsā 70, 74
Jebusites 26
Jehovah 9, 25, 27, 34
Jehovah-nissi 71
Jethro 24, 71 f.
Jochebed 21
Joshua 70, 124

kid 89
Korah 136

laver, the bronze, 115
laws in Exodus 9 ff.
leprosy 29
Levi 14, 121, 138
lex talionis 83
lice 41
locusts 46
LORD = Jehovah 25

McNeile 3, etc.
magicians 37
man, duty of, 9 f.
manna 67 f.
Marah 65
Massah 70
mercy-seat 94
Merenptah 16, 62

Meribah 70
Midian 23, 72
Migdol 58
mighty men (=rams) 64
milk and honey 26
Miriam 29, 64, 70
mitre 107
months, names of, 50
Moses:
  meaning of name 23
  work of 7 f.
  song of 62
mount of God 72
murrain 43

Nadab 36, 90
name, divine, 80, 88
Nile, the, 38

Oholiab 117
oil for lamps 102
omer 69
onycha 116
ovens 39

P 3 f., 18
papyrus 22
parents 78, 82
passover 51
peace-offerings 80
peculiar treasure 75
Pentateuch, authorship of, 1 f.
Perizzite 26
Pharaoh 20
  of oppression 16
  of Exodus 16
Philistines 57
Phinehas 36
Pi-hahiroth 58
pillars 89, 91
Pithom 20
plagues 38 ff.
pomegranates 106
Presence-bread 96
  table of 95
punishments 12, 82

Purasati 16
purple 93
Putiel 36

quails 67

Raamses 20, 54
Rameses II 15 f., 20
  daughters of 22
Red Sea 58
redeem 34
Rephidim 69
Reuel 24
rod, of Moses, 29

Sabbath, the, 78, 117 f.
salt 116
sanctuaries 82
sapphire 105
sardius 104
Sargon of Akkad 22
Sayce 38, 57, 74
scarlet 93
sealskins 93
Seti I 15
shekel 114
Shur 65
Sin, wilderness of, 65
sin offering 109
Sinai 70, 74
slaves 12, 80
Smith, W. Robertson 52, 77, 80, 86
sojourner (=*gêr*) 52
sorceress 85
south (=*negeb*) 98
spoons 95
stacte 116
Succoth 54

tabernacle, the, 13 ff., 93
tables of stone 92, 125
taboo 75
taḥash 93
talent 96
taskmasters 32

Tell el-Amarna tablets 12
Tent of Meeting 102, 123 (*see also* 'tabernacle')
testimony, the, 69, 94
Thothmes III 15
timbrels 64
topaz 104
Torah 1
trumpet 76

unleavened cakes 51

Urim and Thummim 106
usury 86
utterly destroy 85

veil on Moses' face 128
veil of tabernacle 99

Wellhausen 3
west (=sea) 98
Westcott 10, 92
worship 9 ff.